JUST ᵀᴴᴱ TIP

Thank you for
purchasing my book!
I hope you enjoy and
laugh your face off!
♡ - Tonya Frith

JUST THE TIP

TONYA FRITCH

JUST THE TIP
TONYA FRITCH

ISBN: 9798738208386

First edition: April 2020
10 9 8 7 6 5 4 3 2 1

WWW.TONYAFRITCH.COM

Printed and bound in the United States.

DEDICATION

To my parents for having the best sense of humor and making me laugh until I cry. You both inspire and encourage me to make this life what I want it to be and I love you for that.

To never living "a lunchbox life"
-Jano

PREFACE

I started collecting stories of my experiences as a waitress when I was 19. Some of these stories are not about waitressing at all but about a girl, not yet a woman... Ok, ok, these are stories about me, a then 19-year-old waitress who grew up within the service industry. Reading some of this at age 33 makes me cringe about how naïve I was but this was my experience.

INTERVIEW: 4:00PM

INTERVIEWER: "Why do you think we should hire you?"
My mind went blank. I can't believe they threw a trick question at me already.

I looked at the interviewer and then back at the door, quickly glancing between the two quite a few times. The door of the place displayed a large sign on it reading, "We're Hiring!" My eyes started doing that nervous blinking thing, the thing where your eye lashes start fluttering and won't stop, and when it finally does, it only stops in one eye so now it looks like I am profusely winking at the interviewer, possibly ruining my chances of getting hired or worse, encouraging a call to 911. I put my hand over my eye and calmly replied, "I am looking for a job and I noticed you were hiring."

CHAPTER ONE
JUST THE TIP

When I first began serving, nobody could have convinced me that it would be an ongoing career choice for the next ten years. Just to think, if I had dedicated that time to my schooling, I would have a master's degree by now. I would still be serving due to the recent state our economy is in, but everybody respects a waitress who is still in school or has a degree. I was neither, neither in school or respected, and somehow the school thing weighed more on my mind. Instead of dedicating my time to getting a master's degree, I chose to have mastered in minor back problems, hurting feet, and a non-existing savings account.

I always imagined after spending ten years in the same career field that I would feel more accomplished, maybe would have been offered a few raises by now, maybe ten to be exact. Perhaps a promotion was in store. However, I never wanted to be promoted to anything higher than a bartender. After that it seemed like instead of a promotion you got to work endless doubles babysitting your peers, who on any given night are probably making more money than you, but you did get a title. Everybody in the service industry loves a title. Not that I have not seen a promotion, I have gotten promoted to better shifts, therefore making better money, which would be considered a raise for most. If only I could figure out the accomplished part, that would be an accomplishment.

Wait! If you think for one minute that you can write me off as a unaccomplished server who is belittled on a daily basis and who has a job a monkey could do, well, then you would be about 99 percent right, except for the monkey part. See, I'm sure monkeys could perform all the daily serving duties such as bringing food, dropping off and refilling drinks, and cleaning the table after the patrons have left but to deal with the demanding, needy, stuck up, rude, mean looks-as-if-I-have-never-been-in-a-social- setting-before-in-my-life crowd, that requires more than a monkey. Yes, that requires me. I am your tongue-biting, insult-taking, piece-of- shit server. I don't always agree with the piece-of-shit part. I am pretty sure a monkey would scream at the customers if it was being spoken to in a rude tone, or even worse throw their own shit on you if you had belittled their service. I too have wanted to do these exact two things, but we won't go into that just yet.

I'm going to tell you how this all came about. You might be asking yourself, why do I need to read this? I have never served a day in my life. Okay, then, you are exactly who needs to read this. Every server I have ever met has always said that everybody, sometime in their life, should be required to serve. I agree with this completely and think it should be a mandatory course in high school, which you are required to take before entering adulthood. I think the world all together would be a better place if somebody could make this happen, and for everybody else who is already in the "industry" enjoy!

I always wanted to be something "cool" when I grew up. I always thought I was good with people, but it was everything else I knew I needed to work on. I was okay at writing; I was funny in real life. How do I combine the two to do something I love? My current dream job never involved working in the service industry, which I am doing as of now, but this is what all unsure people who want to change the world do. Waiting to do something "better" with your life is common for waiters and waitresses. I decided that while waiting on my dream career to come around, I wanted to write a humorous sort of memoir. Someone needs to write about all the different people I encountered daily for the last ten years. Somewhere, someone out there had to be feeling the same about the situations I was encountering, and some might even find it funny knowing that they are not the only ones who have felt this way. With that being said, I still think I am going to be something "cool" when I grow up.

CHAPTER TWO
WILL THIS HURT? THIS IS MY FIRST TIME.

When I was seventeen years old, that moment came, you know that moment, the one that defines every seventeen-year-old's entry into adulthood? I was terrified and like most teenagers when they are about to experience something new and foreign for the first time, I decided now would be as good as time as any. When my parents came into my room that one summer Sunday evening, I knew exactly what they wanted. They wanted to have "the talk." I knew this day was coming but I never realized how awful it was going to be. They sat on the end of my bed and after awkwardly glancing at each other and then around my room, they said what I hoped to never hear: "It's time for you to get a job." My parents had always helped my brothers and me out when we needed it, but always told us if we wanted extra, we would have to pay for it ourselves. Extra meaning a car, car insurance, and a cell phone. Obviously by the needs that would be provided they meant a place to stay and food to eat. Basically, they vowed they would keep us alive until we reached the ripe age of eighteen. I guess this was fair. Thank you, Mom and Dad.

My mom had worked in restaurants for as long as I can remember. When I was young, I used to love going with my dad to pick her up at all hours of the night. I remember fighting with myself for hours, hoping she would call my dad to pick her up before I fell asleep. I was always a night owl, a reference my dad used quite frequently when describing my sleep habits. Sometimes when we would arrive at her job, she wouldn't be finished yet. We would have to go inside and wait for her to finish her side work. As I sat there waiting, my mom would bring me endless Shirley Temples and my dessert of choice. I remember thinking this is what true joy is. I didn't think life could get better than eating a brownie all the while washing it down with sugared red syrup mixed with Sprite. Now that I think about it, I am filled with pure joy to not have diabetes.

I did struggle with a weight issue in middle school and early high school and just now found my reason why. As I sat at the table, I noticed everything seemed so fast-paced and exciting. People socializing and laughing, music playing, other servers running around smiling (which I now know is a cover up for complete insanity). I was convinced my mom had a good job though and loved seeing her around people; my mom has always been way too nice. I would always hear my mom and dad's conversation in the car on the way home, which included my dad asking my mom how much money she had made that night. Now at this time I knew nothing about tips, or if size mattered, but when she would often tell him "a hundred dollars." At the sound of that, my eyes lit up. I would chime in with ideas on what we should spend this money on, a family vacation, perhaps? My mother would always insist on paying the bills with it instead. She is still like that to this day, and I still opt for vacations instead which could explain my current bank account summary. Obviously, I now know that a hundred dollars is not a lot of money, and most of the time, a hundred dollars doesn't even seem worth it after a ten-hour serving shift.

After the years had gone by and I became a little older and fatter due to the late-night snacking, I tired of brownies and cherry-flavored carbonation and my mom tired of serving people. Something had snapped inside of me one day, and I decided that I never wanted to serve people. I started thinking how absurd it was for somebody to "wait" on you in exchange for money. Not just any money, but what the customer thought was appropriate. It didn't look as exciting as it once had, so you can imagine my disappointment when my mom had suggested that, for my first job, I should work at a restaurant. At first, I was standing my ground. I applied to every bank, fitness club, and grocery store in the area. I avoided any job that involved food, even jobs that offered too long of a lunch break. To my first of many disappointments, I had not been hired at any of these places due to lack of experience. Finally, for kicks, I went into a typical corporate chain restaurant, still refusing to serve. I applied for hostess. A disappointment following a disappointment, I got the job. Apparently, you do not need experience to walk people to a seat and for them to follow your lead and take menus from your hand (yes, this is a real job). This seemed easy enough.

I loved the fact that I only had to say "hi" and "bye" to customers. I had no idea at the time how lucky I truly was to only have to spend seconds, at the most, with the customers, but I quickly learned how unappreciative I was being. Shortly after I started hosting, I noticed servers would come up to me every five minutes complaining about their tables. "Why did you seat me with five kids?" "Really? My table doesn't know how to speak English; do you think they will know how to tip me?" "Great, I just got a seven top of teenagers asking me how much everything cost. Seven isn't enough to add gratuity, and they aren't going to leave me anything!"

Honestly, it didn't matter who I sat where because I would soon realize everybody who came in would suck in their own special, unique way. I started getting upset with servers who were mad at me because people had actually decided to show up to eat that day. I was just glad that even though hosting is one of the most boring jobs imaginable, I wasn't quite as miserable as my co-workers. I don't really remember too many co-workers from that job except for two of them: Vince and Stacey. Vince was our floor manager; he also bartended every night shift of the week. He was tall, dark and handsome. He was 6'4" and had the eight-pack of an airbrushed cover of Men's Health. I only knew this because I had a hugging problem, and instead of my face falling into a soft stomach, I was greeted with eight pultruding lumps of muscle. He was shy about showing his abs though. Now that I think about it, it might have had something to do with our four-year age difference, and I, only being seventeen at the time, can now appreciate him wanting to stay out of my dinner conversations with my parents.

"Yes, Vince, my floor manager is very nice. He is a tall, ripped, African-American. How do I know that he is ripped? He likes to show me his abs." He actually does fitness modeling now and I "like" all his ab pictures on Facebook. Stacey was our TOGO girl, which might reign as most boring job ever. Stacey was quirky and odd. Stacey was about 5'5" with short brown hair and side bangs that she used to cover one side of her face. She wore black thick-rimmed glasses that didn't do a good job at hiding her beautiful brown doe eyes. Her smile was perfect, although I didn't get to see it often at work. She was exactly the kind of person I tend to invite into my life. She was always doing things on her own time and on her own terms. I liked her confidence and we became good friends for a while. Isn't it weird how people come in and out of our lives as easily as the seasons can change? Stacey was only in my life long enough for me to hear her story up until that point, and then she disappeared to start a new chapter in which I was not intended to be a part of. Luckily for them, they aren't still sharing a bartending and TOGO shift with me. I, on the other hand, was on a career path, thinking I would only be working here until the end of the school year, then moving on to a job that was something else altogether. Let me tell you, ten years goes by quick.

One day, when I was working as a hostess, my general manager approached me about serving. He seemed to be approaching the early 40s himself. He was a short, heavier set guy who, judging by his height when standing next to me, came in at a steady 5'4". His black hair was combed slick back over patches of hair that had gone missing due to age or lack of good genetics. He looked like somebody who played a key role in covering up deaths with excuses for the mafia. His gold chain, that I imagine was holding a cross, always hung around his neck, sticking out of a white collared shirt of his choice. He was always nervously smiling when he would walk by you. I heard he had a lot of family issues, mainly with his daughter. I felt like he was extremely unhappy, and I felt bad for him. I never knew if his sadness was caused by his job or his family issues; I assumed both. He wore thin-framed glasses around his very round face that barely covered his black, beady eyes. Still, they were kind eyes. He always anxiously rubbed his hands together when asking employees to do their job as if he wasn't the one in control. When he had approached me about serving, I assured him that I made a better hostess than a server. Being the face of the restaurant and not having to really talk to customers was what I wanted to do.

He told me I had a big personality, and I would be perfect for this kind of job. He told me people would just love me. I'm sure he got my big personality confused with my rather large breasts, and he lied to my face about people loving me. I would soon be theirs to hate. He was using me as prey in a lion's den. I was fresh meat. Too many servers had burned out at the time and decided to move on with their lives. Without knowing it, this is the decision that would affect the next ten years of my life. I soon would be addicted to tips, tips of all sizes.

As with every job, when learning something new, you have to be trained. (Yes, like a monkey.) I know a lot of people question a server's job and how easy it must be. For the most part, they are right. What they can't possibly train you for is the mental and emotional damage that comes with this kind of job. The first few days, you are required to follow around a veteran server (we call them veterans because to stay in this business a certain amount of time, you have basically fought a horrible, unwinnable war). Basically, you have to follow them to the table, stand there awkwardly as they are at the table and watch as the table is looking at you, wondering why you are so closely stalking their server. You just hope your fellow server has not forgotten you and has told their table your reason for being there. This was the easy part. Training, observing, and not having to be the center of attention. At this point, you are not the reason why everything went horribly wrong, single handily ruining this table's entire day. My trainer had mentioned that it would not be rare to find myself or another co-worker crying in the walk-in freezer while looking for a condiment we ran out of. I thought he was kidding. I could not imagine a job as easy as this making you cry, and I thought the other waitresses he had used as examples were weak. I didn't know of anybody breaking down at work, unless a broken heart or alcohol is involved. I know this may seem like a dramatic statement but what I didn't realize yet is how soon one can forget the simplicity of one's job when your mental state is being tested on a daily basis.

By the time training was over, I felt confident in myself that I would do just fine on the floor if not better than the person who had trained me. My trainer was this guy in his mid-20s who was maybe 5'6" when he wore dress shoes with a heel. He liked to spend his money on vices rather than bills, and he always seemed untrustworthy to me. He later told all the servers he would do all their side work for $5 a pop so that they could get out early. He got around $100 off them before quitting the job without doing any of the work he had promised. I, maybe being the only one, thought it was a very smart way to quit. I wondered if I would ever get to the point of quitting in a brilliant way such as he did but I also wonder if he is in jail now.

They only gave you two table sections when first starting at this restaurant and I thought, how hard this could possibly be. I could not have been more wrong. This happened often. I never had anticipated how awkward it would be to approach complete strangers on an hourly basis. As I sat my first few tables, I didn't make the three second rule. The three second rule meaning you, as a server, have 3 seconds after the customer sits down to greet them. I was too nervous to approach my table right when they sat down, preparing myself from afar. I would watch them and try to figure out if they looked like friendly people, if they were out for a special occasion that I had the potential of messing up, or if the husband was already pissed off because his wife couldn't cook. I would soon realize that I couldn't prepare myself for my tables because they were all going to be different: from the way they looked, to the way they talked. I started questioning how I could anticipate so many peoples' wants and needs with only so many hours in a shift and with only one of me. I don't know why I pondered this for so long because I didn't have a choice on whether I could or could not approach the table. I was putting off the inevitable, which only led me to one thing: I approached my first table. My first table was a middle-aged couple with two young children. One was a toddler around two and the other just a baby. At this point in my life, I thought children were cute. At the time, I had no idea I would later be diagnosed with a rare allergy to children. Now, I can't go within ten feet of children without getting anxious or possibly breaking out in hives. My doctor assures me this is not a real disease and says it's all in my head. Either way, with no medicine and no cure, I cannot take that chance and these days tell the hostess to sit kids in other servers' sections due to my serious medical condition. They don't bother to question me about this and I don't bother sharing. However, prior to being unofficially diagnosed, this seemed to be a great first table.

"Hi, how are you guys doing today? My name is—"

"Do you guys have a kids menu?" the mother said, interrupting. "We need to put their food in first because they haven't eaten all day and will start crying." I pointed to the menu on the table and showed them the section that read Kids Menu while wondering to myself why their kids had not eaten all day. After I pointed out the options we offered for kids, the mom asked me if we had spaghetti. I was very thrown off by this because clearly, out of the five items we offered for kids, spaghetti was not one of them. She made me question my whole menu training and wondered if I, myself, had studied the wrong kids menu. I was also left wondering why food was even in question when I had yet to receive their drink orders. I ignored her initial question and asked what they would like to drink, after asking me what kind of drinks we had; I noticed I had been sat with another table three minutes prior. I was getting anxious and didn't anticipate a greeting taking ten minutes. My other table was looking around for their server, not knowing it was me, the girl who looked like she had all the time in the world to give to this one family. I finally got the two waters and two kid milk orders that they took way too long to decide on and went up to my next table to start my spiel that I had been interrupted on the first time.

"Hi, how are you guys doing today?" I asked my second table.

"We are doing well, how are you?" This was so much better of a start than the last table, so I decided to continue with my greeting.

"My name is Tonya, I will be helping you guys out today. What can I get you guys to drink?"

"Do you have a gluten free menu?" My face just fell. Why was this drink thing so difficult? Who didn't anticipate getting their drink first while dining out? I thought it was sort of a known rule. To be honest, I wasn't even sure what gluten was at the time and felt like I could just make something up and they would have to believe me, being their all-knowing server. I offered a pasta dish, being that I love pasta. They looked at me in horror.

"We can't have pasta that could kill us!"

After accusing me of attempted murder, I suddenly became very annoyed. How was I supposed to know what this lady could and couldn't eat? Has she not been dealing with this allergy most or all of her life? I had only been dealing with this for five minutes and I was supposed to be the expert? I couldn't believe how within two tables everybody's problem had become mine. My trainer had not mentioned the extra baggage that was to be handled and it definitely wasn't in the handbook I had received and signed after being hired.

Now the kids at the other table started to cry. The parents looked pissed, as if I had forgotten them. I ran back to the kitchen and asked the cooks what was gluten free. I found out that basically all of our dishes could be gluten free if only 99 percent of the ingredients were taken out. At this restaurant, we had a salad bar and I opted to recommend that instead. They were not so pleased. After all, salad sucked. I understood and was thankful that I did not have gluten allergies. With the salad bar and two waters rang in, I was basically in the clear from one table but dreaded going back to the first table. I put a smile on and approached the table with their drinks. I knew they were upset. They weren't looking at me and they weren't smiling. I just stood there like a scolded child who knew I had done bad. They quickly gave me their food orders and I quickly walked away, hoping my shift was already almost over. The table eventually got their "mediocre" food, or so they called it, right before the left me a "mediocre" tip.

I had three more tables stagger in throughout my shift after what seemed like hours apart and all ran up low tabs since the menu itself included very reasonable prices. My tips seemed more than unreasonable. At the time, I was just excited to take home cash, no matter how much it was. At the end of my shift, I had to print out a server report, which told me how much I made in credit card tips and how much I owed or was owed in cash at the end of the night. My sales were low, and my tips were lower. I was about to walk out with $34 when my boss thought this would be a good time to inform me about tip out. Tip out are funds that restaurants don't want to pay to other workers, so they get other employees to chip in to pay for their services. At this place of employment, we had to tip out the salad bar attendant for restocking the salad bar and the busser. I didn't see how the salad bar had anything to do with my tips, and since we had been so slow and I only had six tables in a seven hour shift, I had plenty of opportunity to bus all of my tables myself. I didn't agree to give my hard-earned tips to people who had not dealt with gluten allergies or mediocre personalities. There was nothing I could do about it and after I found out I couldn't single handily change the way tip out was going to work here, I walked out with my twenty five dollars almost in tears. I lived thirty minutes away at the time and was pretty sure my gas tank needed a refill. That was going to be the most pointless shift in my working career. Or it was until the next day at work.

The thing is, it is really hard to stay motivated and stay dedicated to showing up to a job everyday where you aren't even guaranteed pay. That is why the serving turnover rate is high and endless. When somebody told me that all serving required was for me to do a good job to guarantee a good tip, it sounded too good to be true. As with all good things, it was. It doesn't even matter how hard you work; you can be a great server, timely and personable, but the only thing that matters in the end is what kind of mood your table is in, what kind of job they have, and what was or was not in their bank account that week under the account titled, "just giving away." I like to think people tip more based on their personality, the taste of their food, and the content of alcohol they have in their drinks, all of which I have nothing to do with, so it would be hard for me to convince them that somehow I still deserved a small fee for saying hello and taking their plates to the kitchen when they were finished eating. Honestly, money has nothing to do with it; the reason why people have more money than others to begin with is because they don't like to spend it. I have waited on a large variety of customers, ranging from homeless people who didn't even pay for their meal rather alone leave me a tip to doctors and lawyers who also didn't tip. I have had people tell me they had so much money they could buy this town. They were the same people who would pull out a stack of hundreds and somewhere in the middle, after thumbing through the hundreds the third time as I wait there for my tip, as I was asked to do, like a puppy in training ("stayyyyyyyy"), they find a five dollar bill. Oh my God. Thank you so much, you kind, kind sir. Now if only you had at least tipped me twenty percent of your bill, then you would have something to feel good about. My point being, after a $25 dollar shift the night before, my morale isn't exactly skyrocketing while driving to work the next day.

As I'm walking into work the following evening, I can't help but have thoughts of wanting to run back to my car. I turn around to look; it is too far. I show up to work at four o'clock. Four o'clock is usually a good shift; it allows you to wait on all the tables for an hour before your other co-workers show up. At this particular place, it gave you the chance to stand around for two hours and think long and hard why you even bothered showing up for a shift where you stand around for two hours and don't get paid. I never came up with an answer good enough to justify quitting. That's because as soon as I was sure I was quitting, I would have a really good shift that concluded with excellent tips. That day, my tables were tipping me decent, and we managed to pull in a nice dinner rush. I had made near a hundred dollars in seven hours, and after picking up my friend who worked in retail across the street after work that night, her one hundred and fifty dollar a week job seemed very unreasonable. I completely forgot about my shift from the night before. This went on for the next few months (or years, but who's counting?), a few horrible days in a row and one good day as if to say thanks for hanging in there and to trick you into thinking your job doesn't suck as bad as you think it does. I managed to focus on the good nights for the most part and forget about the bad, but sometimes my bills didn't allow me to forget that I didn't have enough in my bank account to pay them. One Friday night, I couldn't take it anymore.

I was that girl crying in the walk-in freezer while looking for ranch for the salad bar attendant who I was tipping out, who was having me go look for his ranch. Let me go back an hour and explain why I had become another emotional casualty. I was getting pretty good at my job by this point, and the manager started trusting me with larger parties. That night, I was getting sat with my first eight top. I promptly set their table, already excited to pick up their tips in an hour before they had even arrived. In order to take this party, I had to give up my early out shift and stay to close. For only being in high school, this job was sure putting a damper on my nonexistent social life on the weekends. It was a Friday night that I would have rather spent in the Wendy's parking lot across the street with friends. My friends and I were easily entertained, and, plus, I loved fries. After being thirty minutes late, my eight top finally sat down.

"Hi, how are you guys doing today?" No answer.

I'm pretty sure even a few of them made eye contact with me and didn't say anything. One of the ladies even started a new conversation as I stood there, invisible. What was going on? I tried to put my hand through my other hand, only to realize it was still a solid object, which meant the rest of me had to still be a solid, existing object as well. After standing asking them one more time how they were doing, without one of them even fluttering an eye at me, I decided to break out into a front handspring on the table, and as I was doing a back flip off the other end, I noticed that one lady had not even looked up from her menu. I then retracted my back flip and landed in her lap.

"Ma'am, what would you like to drink?" I asked, as I straddled her. "Will you please withhold your conversation until I am done taking your orders?"

She looked right through me. How could she not feel the weight of my ass on her bony knees? She replied simply by saying to her friend, "Can you believe after all these years Rebecca is going to get married?"

"WE WILL ALL HAVE WATERS!" I was abruptly interrupted from my daydream and wasn't quite sure if this was the first time, they were answering my question. I was sure I had been standing there for what felt like five long minutes. Do you know how long a couple of minutes feel when you are standing in front of eight strangers, who are all ignoring you? The eight waters didn't lighten the blow whatsoever. I arrived minutes later with their waters. One of the ladies asked me if I could bring them lemons for their water. It was not until about the third trip of bringing lemons back to the table did I notice the lady making her own lemonade for free. I hated this table already. When asked what they would like to eat, I received four food orders with the request for four extra empty plates for sharing. I went into the kitchen and into the freezer and started taking deep breaths. That's when it happened, what I thought would never happen, not to me at least. Tears started flowing. I wish I could have seen myself when one of the cooks who didn't speak English had opened the freezer to get some ingredients only to see me, standing there looking at him, crying. He got his ingredients and closed the door. I appreciated that he had enough sense to know that I obviously needed some time to myself. I would have done the same thing for him.

I went to my general manager, pleading with him to let me go home and let these assholes fend for themselves. I was even about to recommend the Wendy's across the street where I wanted to be, that way all eight of them could have ordered dinner for the price of the four entrees they scraped together. No manager would put up with this kind of behavior. I was digging myself a grave that I didn't mind sleeping in, but to my surprise, he told me I could leave. Unsure if that meant permanently, I asked him if he was joking. He said, "No, I will have somebody cover the rest of your shift. Enjoy your night." This doesn't happen in real life, and I am glad I got to experience this once at a place of employment before I die. I high-booked my ass out of there. I later found out that the waiter who had taken over had to stay an extra thirty minutes after close and was basically stiffed out of any sort of tip. I didn't make it much longer there. Aside from the convenient location to Wendy's, it wasn't enough. A few weeks later, I found myself yelling at a table for leaving me a 73 cent tip on a credit card slip. Why even bother at all! My manager told me that the way I acted was no way to interact with tables, even though I assured him he didn't want these clients as repeat customers, anyway. A few days later, a guy came in and short changed me about hundred dollars without me even realizing it until the end of my shift when, not only did my report show I didn't make any money at the end of the night, but that I owed the restaurant eight dollars from my pocket. We later looked at the security cameras after I told the manager about the weird guy I had encountered earlier in the night and saw him running across the parking lot at a highly immoral speed on the monitor. To this day I won't give anybody who is not at one of my tables change and will never count change in front of somebody. Shortly after, I followed a fellow employee's advice who said she was leaving to go to a bigger corporation in a nicer area. Sure, the drive would be almost an hour from my house, but certainly larger tips would be more enjoyable. The last night of work, I told every server I would do their side work for five dollars... That didn't happen. I didn't have the guts. I just never showed up to work again.

He also had monthly probation visits and drug tests. One day when he had decided today would be a good day to come to work on drugs, his probation officer called his color in for testing. He decided not to go in for it because he would fail. They arrested him at work the next day. Fail. I met Jane, the bar slut, not my words everybody else's, and C.J. who thought that we were all experimental aliens under government supervision with the main purpose of making gold. Yes, I too thought this guy was a little off but it turned out he was just high all the time, and after giving him the chance to explain everything, I too thought this could be a possibility and it was a better answer than I had come up with relating to our existence. The fact that so many different people, who were not afraid to voice their opinions 24 hours a day, and I had to work under the same roof together brought fighting, arguing, love, and cheating. Really, the only thing servers usually have in common is their love for quick cash. Most servers hate their job, and they are all waiting for something better to come along.

After I went through the basics of training, as I had with my previous serving job, I started with food running shifts to help me learn my table numbers. When I started at this restaurant, we were running a themed menu that required us all to wear Hawaiian shirts. I remember mine being very ugly and not Hawaiian at all. I had in fact found it in the old lady's department at J.C. Penny. It was just a normal black button up shirt with huge orange flowers on it. I found it very slimming, and just for kicks, I purchased a mustard yellow shirt with dull pink flowers on it from the same department store. Both were equally disgusting. Food running meant I had to take a huge tray that could hold up to six plates at a time, carry it over my head, grab a tray stand with my free hand and make it to the table spill free. I would like to say I nailed this the first time, but I would be lying. More than once did my tray does not make it to the table and more than once did the food reach the table before I or the tray did. People were mad that their food was on the ground and servers were mad at me for costing them their tip. I apologized for not being perfect and told them I would work on that "human flaw" thing.

After a while, I was moved to the next part of my training, which meant I had to spend time as the SA. SA stood for salad attendant. What is up with these places and their need for attending to salads all the time? This job was easy but always kind of embarrassing. It was clearly a job for a rookie or for somebody who didn't speak English. You were not required to talk, only to make countless salads according to their modifications. The only part I liked about SA was the free breadsticks we were supposed to give out that I mostly gave out to myself. I had not signed up for back of the house duties; after all, my whole calling in life was to serve people (I had to tell myself this on several occasions).

One day when I was babysitting the salads, I noticed a guy in the kitchen in street clothes picking up a paycheck from the back. Every single girl must have come up to him to give him a hug. I wanted one too, but with the whole not knowing each other thing, I thought that, unless I wanted a permanent job as SA, I should keep my hands to my salad. I figured he must have been picking up his last paycheck because I had not seen him here up until that day. He was attractive and I was smitten. Even with my hideous knock-off Hawaiian shirt, I thought I had caught his eye. The thought never crossed my mind that the giant orange flowers on my shirt might have made it hard to keep anybody's attention from me. No sooner than this thought crossed my mind, he came up to me, complimenting my taste in shirts. I knew he was lying but accepted the sarcastic compliment and went back to tossing my salad.

A few days later, he, who I eventually found out went by the name of Richard, showed up to work in his equally awful shirt. Okay, maybe not equal, his looked decent. Mine was awful. He already had an exotic look and the shirt looked like something he had just pulled from his Polynesian closet. I was more focused on what he would look like with a lack of shirt than the actual design on it. I was only nineteen at the time and he was twenty-two. Richard had a natural olive skin tone, dark brown hair and brown eyes. He was about 5'11" according to him and had these thick brown eyebrows that ladies adored. You could tell he worked out. He was incredibly toned and, from the looks of how women acted around him, was apparently everybody's type. In my first few weeks there, he would constantly make conversation around me, about me, but never directed it at me. He would tell everybody in ear range that he thought I was attractive and joked about how he wouldn't mind getting to know me better. I was very rude at first; I don't know why exactly. It was like I had personality Tourette's. I would want to say something witty and funny back but a disgusted look on my face showed up instead. One day he even asked me if I knew English and he didn't smile. I didn't smile. A lot of people have asked if I am of Latin descent. I am not. Oh, and I know English, despite what my ugly Hawaiian shirt and salad bar attendant job title may be screaming at you. I was just playing hard to get, and it was working.

One day, Richard asked me to come hang out with him at his house after work. I managed to say, "Sure." As I was waiting for him to get off work, possibly every female who worked there decided to stop by and give me some advice on my very near future date. They all told me not to hang out with him and that he simply was inviting me over to sleep with him. Somehow, he had forgotten to mention this part to me. I was a virgin and planned to remain that way until—insert weakness here " Yes, this once seemed like a very attainable goal. Word traveled fast; nobody could believe I was nineteen and still a virgin. Who was I kidding? Up until that point, I had only kissed one guy. Waiting until marriage started to seem very unrealistic to me when I found out what hormones were. I still decided to hang out with Richard that night, and to my surprise, I lost my virginity. No. I am kidding. What kind of girl do you take me for? We made food and he note-booked me. Note-booked is when a guy is trying to seduce you by watching The Notebook with you. This time it didn't work but thanks to Nicholas Sparks' many book-to-movie accomplishments, I imagined it was only a matter of time before he was able to seduce me with a romantic movie. The next day went fine until my female co-workers described my date to me in detail before I or Richard even had the chance to say anything. What was up with this guy? Could he not come up with any new material? I decided to start focusing on tips that could buy me things instead of tips that could give me things.

The longer I worked at this corporate restaurant, the better sections I started to get. Smoking and cocktail sections were the best. Second-hand smoke always bothered me but who was worried about your lungs filling up with smoke, when you had $100 in cash to take home on a nightly basis? At nineteen, I wasn't. We had a lot of regulars come into this place, which was good because most of them tipped you well, knowing that they were more than likely going to be seeing you on a weekly basis.

I soon found out that Saturdays were the worst nights to work. When I had first started there, Richard told me to tell them that I couldn't work Saturday nights and that he even made up a fake job he didn't have at Abercrombie, which he happened only to work at on Saturdays, to get out of Saturdays at the bar. Being so new there, I didn't think I was obligated to tell them when I could or couldn't work, besides how bad could it be? I soon found out. It was bad enough for somebody to make up a fake job. The restaurant was located in the same shopping center as a movie theater, and it seemed that everybody chose Saturday nights to go out and watch them, making our place a perfect pit stop before or after their movie. We were always busy on these nights, but it was the wrong kind of busy. Saturdays consisted of young teenagers without jobs and people who refused to take off their sunglasses, even though it was night. We even played "I Wear my Sunglasses at Night" multiple times every Saturday night. It became an inside joke between the staff. Instead of customers finding it offensive, they seemed like they quite enjoyed it. Then there were the women. Being a female myself, it may sound offensive, but these particular women hardly ever tipped well. In fact, when handing the bill back to the man who paid at a table, seeing the women take the book to write in a tip made my stomach churn, and I assume the people who wear sunglasses at night don't tip because they clearly can't see where to write the tip in. We used to refer to our customers on Saturdays as motorboats. Motorboats don't tip and neither did they. Saturdays were bad and I was jealous that Richard got to work at his "other job" on these days. I wondered what he did with those nights off and how many other girls were in line to be note-booked.

CHAPTER THREE
WOULD YOU LIKE YOUR SALAD TOSSED?

I decided to wait until high school was over before applying for another job that required me to leave at midnight and then get up at 6 am. Not even a week after graduating, I applied to a bigger corporate chain restaurant and got hired after insisting I speak to a manager during a dinner rush as I myself had plans and needed to get out of there. By the way, don't ever be that asshole. This restaurant was more "grown up" than the last place I had worked. As with most restaurants, it's not strange to see multiple love affairs, sexual relations, or some might even call them relationships. Restaurants and bars provide the atmosphere to socialize with people of the opposite gender, and it is no different if you're on the clock. At my first serving job, I didn't try to know what exactly was going on with people and their dating status, but it seemed pretty inevitable that people here felt like I should know everybody's business. One of my first days there, I was introduced to Linda. Linda was a heavier set African-American woman who I was told had taken a liking to stealing cucumbers from our kitchen on numerous occasions, always seeming to choose the largest cucumbers. I'm not one to make assumptions, but obviously her love for cucumber salad at home was getting a bit ridiculous. I met Chris, who was a younger guy with longer blonde hair, a baby face with a crooked smile. His teeth weren't bad; they were shorter as if he spent his nights grinding them in his sleep. Chris was nice and I took a liking to him. I later found out that he was addicted to pain pills, even though I was quite sure he was in no pain. There was even a time when he asked me if I had anything above my sink that he could take. Sure that he could not get high off of my toothpaste, I decided to offer it to him anyways and he sadly declined.

He also had monthly probation visits and drug tests. One day when he had decided today would be a good day to come to work on drugs, his probation officer called his color in for testing. He decided not to go in for it because he would fail. They arrested him at work the next day. Fail. I met Jane, the bar slut, not my words everybody else's, and C.J. who thought that we were all experimental aliens under government supervision with the main purpose of making gold. Yes, I too thought this guy was a little off but it turned out he was just high all the time, and after giving him the chance to explain everything, I too thought this could be a possibility and it was a better answer than I had come up with relating to our existence. The fact that so many different people, who were not afraid to voice their opinions 24 hours a day, and I had to work under the same roof together brought fighting, arguing, love, and cheating. Really, the only thing servers usually have in common is their love for quick cash. Most servers hate their job, and they are all waiting for something better to come along.

After I went through the basics of training, as I had with my previous serving job, I started with food running shifts to help me learn my table numbers. When I started at this restaurant, we were running a themed menu that required us all to wear Hawaiian shirts. I remember mine being very ugly and not Hawaiian at all. I had in fact found it in the old lady's department at J.C. Penny. It was just a normal black button up shirt with huge orange flowers on it. I found it very slimming, and just for kicks, I purchased a mustard yellow shirt with dull pink flowers on it from the same department store. Both were equally disgusting. Food running meant I had to take a huge tray that could hold up to six plates at a time, carry it over my head, grab a tray stand with my free hand and make it to the table spill free. I would like to say I nailed this the first time, but I would be lying. More than once did my tray does not make it to the table and more than once did the food reach the table before I or the tray did. People were mad that their food was on the ground and servers were mad at me for costing them their tip. I apologized for not being perfect and told them I would work on that "human flaw" thing.

After a while, I was moved to the next part of my training, which meant I had to spend time as the SA. SA stood for salad attendant. What is up with these places and their need for attending to salads all the time? This job was easy but always kind of embarrassing. It was clearly a job for a rookie or for somebody who didn't speak English. You were not required to talk, only to make countless salads according to their modifications. The only part I liked about SA was the free breadsticks we were supposed to give out that I mostly gave out to myself. I had not signed up for back of the house duties; after all, my whole calling in life was to serve people (I had to tell myself this on several occasions).

One day when I was babysitting the salads, I noticed a guy in the kitchen in street clothes picking up a paycheck from the back. Every single girl must have come up to him to give him a hug. I wanted one too, but with the whole not knowing each other thing, I thought that, unless I wanted a permanent job as SA, I should keep my hands to my salad. I figured he must have been picking up his last paycheck because I had not seen him here up until that day. He was attractive and I was smitten. Even with my hideous knock-off Hawaiian shirt, I thought I had caught his eye. The thought never crossed my mind that the giant orange flowers on my shirt might have made it hard to keep anybody's attention from me. No sooner than this thought crossed my mind, he came up to me, complimenting my taste in shirts. I knew he was lying but accepted the sarcastic compliment and went back to tossing my salad.

A few days later, he, who I eventually found out went by the name of Richard, showed up to work in his equally awful shirt. Okay, maybe not equal, his looked decent. Mine was awful. He already had an exotic look and the shirt looked like something he had just pulled from his Polynesian closet. I was more focused on what he would look like with a lack of shirt than the actual design on it. I was only nineteen at the time and he was twenty-two. Richard had a natural olive skin tone, dark brown hair and brown eyes. He was about 5'11" according to him and had these thick brown eyebrows that ladies adored. You could tell he worked out. He was incredibly toned and, from the looks of how women acted around him, was apparently everybody's type. In my first few weeks there, he would constantly make conversation around me, about me, but never directed it at me. He would tell everybody in ear range that he thought I was attractive and joked about how he wouldn't mind getting to know me better. I was very rude at first; I don't know why exactly. It was like I had personality Tourette's. I would want to say something witty and funny back but a disgusted look on my face showed up instead. One day he even asked me if I knew English and he didn't smile. I didn't smile. A lot of people have asked if I am of Latin descent. I am not. Oh, and I know English, despite what my ugly Hawaiian shirt and salad bar attendant job title may be screaming at you. I was just playing hard to get, and it was working. One day, Richard asked me to come hang out with him at his house after work. I managed to say, "Sure." As I was waiting for him to get off work, possibly every female who worked there decided to stop by and give me some advice on my very near future date. They all told me not to hang out with him and that he simply was inviting me over to sleep with him. Somehow, he had forgotten to mention this part to me. I was a virgin and planned to remain that way until—insert weakness here " Yes, this once seemed like a very attainable goal. Word traveled fast; nobody could believe I was nineteen and still a virgin. Who was I kidding? Up until that point, I had only kissed one guy. Waiting until marriage started to seem very unrealistic to me when I found out what hormones were. I still decided to hang out with Richard that night, and to my surprise, I lost my virginity. No. I am kidding. What kind of girl do you take me for? We made food and he note-booked me. Note-booked is when a guy is trying to seduce you by watching The Notebook with you. This time it didn't work but thanks to Nicholas Sparks' many book-to-movie accomplishments, I imagined it was only a matter of time before he was able to seduce me with a romantic movie. The next day went fine until my female co-workers described my date to me in detail before I or Richard even had the chance to say anything. What was up with this guy? Could he not come up with any new material? I decided to start focusing on tips that could buy me things instead of tips that could give me things.

The longer I worked at this corporate restaurant, the better sections I started to get. Smoking and cocktail sections were the best. Second-hand smoke always bothered me but who was worried about your lungs filling up with smoke, when you had $100 in cash to take home on a nightly basis? At nineteen, I wasn't. We had a lot of regulars come into this place, which was good because most of them tipped you well, knowing that they were more than likely going to be seeing you on a weekly basis.

I soon found out that Saturdays were the worst nights to work. When I had first started there, Richard told me to tell them that

I couldn't work Saturday nights and that he even made up a fake job he didn't have at Abercrombie, which he happened only to work at on Saturdays, to get out of Saturdays at the bar. Being so new there, I didn't think I was obligated to tell them when I could or couldn't work, besides how bad could it be? I soon found out. It was bad enough for somebody to make up a fake job. The restaurant was located in the same shopping center as a movie theater, and it seemed that everybody chose Saturday nights to go out and watch them, making our place a perfect pit stop before or after their movie. We were always busy on these nights, but it was the wrong kind of busy. Saturdays consisted of young teenagers without jobs and people who refused to take off their sunglasses, even though it was night. We even played "I Wear my Sunglasses at Night" multiple times every Saturday night. It became an inside joke between the staff. Instead of customers finding it offensive, they seemed like they quite enjoyed it. Then there were the women. Being a female myself, it may sound offensive, but these particular women hardly ever tipped well. In fact, when handing the bill back to the man who paid at a table, seeing the women take the book to write in a tip made my stomach churn, and I assume the people who wear sunglasses at night don't tip because they clearly can't see where to write the tip in. We used to refer to our customers on Saturdays as motorboats. Motorboats don't tip and neither did they. Saturdays were bad and I was jealous that Richard got to work at his "other job" on these days. I wondered what he did with those nights off and how many other girls were in line to be note-booked.

JUST THE TIP

CHAPTER FOUR
TIS' THE SEASON TO NOT TIP

Within six months of working at that corporation, the holidays were rearing their obnoxious heads. Don't get me wrong, I love the holidays, especially Christmas. What I don't love is how unlovely people are around Christmas. I'm sure at one time, it was a very "jolly" season where people would exchange a gift with somebody whom they cared deeply about, or better yet, one time it was considered Jesus's birthday. Oh no, but not anymore. It's not about having one special gift, it's about having many pointless ones. It's about eating so much food that our obesity rate goes up a percent. It's about selfish people not wanting to share money for presents on tipping. Don't get me wrong, Christmas is also a time in many restaurants where you make a lot of money from the sheer volume of Christmas shoppers. Christmas time seems to bring a particular breed out. They are an unpleasant, demanding, angry, and tired breed, all while trying to keep a smile on their face while telling you to have a blessed holiday as they leave their table filled with small blessed tips.

One day, around this wonderful holiday, I had a table that I remember quite well. It was a family that consisted of two kids, an overweight, stressed-out dad, and his timid wife. We were very busy. It was a day shift and my restaurant was located about three minutes from the largest shopping mall in that area. People flooded in around this time of year for lunch because they needed to take a lunch break from Christmas shopping. I welcomed the busyness with ease and couldn't wait to take home the money that I too would be spending on Christmas gifts for loved ones. As I approached the family of four, I could already tell the dad is not having a good day. Why would he, I thought. He and his wife obviously lost the flame after she lost her figure after having to bear two children out a hole no bigger than a quarter. Thank God, I haven't had to figure that one out yet. I approached the table with caution as if I were at a petting zoo; I even thought to stick out my hand for them to sniff me out first. As soon as I approached the table, I was greeted with "We are starving, and we need our food as quickly as possible."

I was glad I decided not to put my hand out and quickly took the food and drink orders. As I said before, we were extremely busy that day. The whole place was full, and we were on a thirty-minute wait for food. Tickets in the kitchen were running slower than usual or getting lost. As a customer, when I go out to eat, I am fully aware that if a restaurant is busy, I will have to wait longer for my food. I also understand that my server is only a human being (unfortunately), who only has human being skills and feelings. This table, like many tables, obviously did not share my understanding. As I was waiting for their food to come, I was greeting other tables and fulfilling my serving responsibilities to them when the dad at my unhappy table of four started yelling my name across the room while I was talking to another customer.

I ignored him up until he started throwing Christmas ornaments from our Christmas tree that was on display near his table. Did this guy just throw an ornament at me? I'm pretty sure I just got hit by a round, glittery blue ball.

I went up to him, cutting off my table that I had been talking to, to tell him he could not throw inanimate objects at his server. He then got an attitude with me and asked where his food was. At this point, I was livid. I wanted to throw his laughing kids across the room as he had done with the decorations and replied with, "I don't know where your food is because I am not cooking it!" He then asked me how I could possibly know when his food was ready if I was out here greeting other tables and not in the kitchen waiting. It kills me to hear the lack of knowledge people have about restaurants when they eat out. I told him that when his food was ready, a food runner would bring it out. Probably not knowing what a food runner was and mad that I had an answer for his question, he became very angry and started cussing at me in front of everybody in my section. I went to my manager and told her I felt completely disrespected and that this man was throwing ornaments at me for God's sake! After talking to the table when their microwaved food was delivered, she came up to me, furious.

Was this really happening??!?! I now think that I should have thrown ornaments back at him. It was official. I had turned into a robot server for a corporation that thought my respect and feelings should be left at home. She then interrupted my thought process with lingering words of possibly being fired for yelling at a customer. Should I remind her of the ornament incident one more time? Perhaps not. It may have been my only argument, but I was pretty sure it was good one. I then thought my next job should be a babysitter; it was basically the same thing: feeding them, giving them drinks, and maybe one day offering complimentary ass wipes. Oh, and the best part, babies can't talk back. Just then a young couple came up to my manager and told her that she was completely in the wrong and that they couldn't stand to watch me get disciplined over an asshole like that. I had not known it, but they had witnessed the whole ornament ordeal, and I was shocked that they had cared enough to tell my 'customer is always right' manager that in fact, this time, the customer was wrong. The look on her face was priceless; she went from a Pitbull to a Matisse. I could not wait to hear what she had to say when the couple left. When they walked away, she gave me a halfhearted smile, said a meaningless, quick sorry, and then told me to get back to work. NOT HOW I SAW THAT HAPPENING! I was waiting for an apology. Check. My manager smiled. Check. Her smile could have been a bit more apologetic, but I realized there was no use in crying over broken ornaments, and I went back to work.

My double that I had signed up for was over in seven hours...as my eleven-hour shift was coming to an end, I hardly remembered my morning shift, which suddenly seemed like days ago. This shift developed problem after problem, complaint after complaint, and soon. Instead of my manager threatening to fire servers who weren't making customers happy, she started making excuses as to why she couldn't make table visits. I understood. Who would want to fight in a hopeless battle? I managed to complete my side work and limp out of work. You may think I am exaggerating but try standing on your feet for forty-plus hours a week. We even have to eat standing up, and due to my germophobic tendencies, I even pee standing up in my place of employment. My old hand-me-down couch was like heaven when I got home.

JUST THE TIP

CHAPTER FIVE

IT'S ABOUT TO GET INTIMATE!

I had just arrived home to my barely livable apartment when Richard had decided to call me, asking me to come over. We had this thing at work where we didn't talk to each other. Most people might call that being ignored. Ok, I was being ignored but we had been seeing each other 'not so seriously' for about seven months, and I was starting to think it was more serious for me than him. Even if my co-workers had been able to predict my first few dates, none of them had predicted that we would still be seeing each other past that. As tired as I was, I looked around my empty apartment with no cable and decided it was a perfect excuse to make my way over. Who needed sleep anyway? I was already counting down until my next double shift when I arrived. It was five hours away. Richard and I both worked a lot at this time. I'm pretty sure there was an entire week when I didn't wash my hair due to lack of sleep and time. I even slept in my work clothes to save time. It may sound strange, but an extra fifteen minutes of sleep went a long way in those days. I got scared when my hair started to dread because I couldn't imagine eventually having to shave my head completely. Thankfully, Herbal Essences was everything it is promised to be.

Richard's house was odd. It was very suitable for him, though, because he was odd. He based almost everything in life on astrological signs and readings, reading everybody as if they were a page from a book (literally). He lived in a four-bedroom house with three other co-workers. He had made the downstairs living room into his bedroom. The kitchen was disgusting, and the appliances were very outdated. What seemed like five inches of dust covered everything. I personally felt like food should not be consumed at all in this house. It was Thaun's parents' house. Thaun was Richard's best friend. They even believed they were each other's soulmates, even though Thaun had a girlfriend. Thaun was Vietnamese, bald, and of medium build. He always had interesting artwork that would permanently cover his body in the form of tattoos and he sometimes wore black, thick-rimmed glasses. Thaun was wise for his time; this was before hipsters were a defined thing. He worked with us as a bartender. Thaun's parents were letting him live and rent out the house until they decided to sell it. It was his childhood home, but I am sure it looked nothing like it did back then. He turned the foyer into his painting room. Canvases lay on their stands and on the ground. Unfinished art was always the center of attention when you walked in. Most of the art had been painted over four or five times. He was an excellent artist and I loved his portraits, even though he hated them. The house was not lacking in character and certainly neither were the characters who lived there. Thaun and his girlfriend Abigail lived upstairs. Abigail was a bubbly, blonde—sometimes red and one time bald (by choice)—teenager who also worked with us as a hostess. She was about 5'5", medium build, with decent boobs, a small waist, and a touch of love handles where she let her jeans hug her. I don't know who came up with the term love handles, considering nobody I have ever talked to love the way they were handling anything. I loved how strange and entertaining Thaun and Abigail were together. You could tell that Abigail was completely in love with Thaun, and after she got a permanent cartoon portrait of him and her on her entire back, I was even surer of it. Thaun had an art degree but chose to bartend instead, and Abigail was also dabbling in classes at the time. For what, I am not sure, and come to think of it, I don't think I ever asked. They were probably the most animated couple I have had the pleasure of seeing in real life. Of course, they had their problems, but even their fights just felt like an excuse to make up afterwards.

This was a memorable time for me because, up until this point, I was used to being overprotected. Hanging out with these eccentric people with these untraditional ways of thinking had me realizing that my life was just beginning. My dad on the other hand was trying to protect my innocence for as long as possible. He once told me, if he could go back, he would have probably chosen to not have kids in general. Meaning, he would have chosen to not have me exist, not knowing me at the time of course, and only because it takes up, well, your entire life. I understand that he doesn't feel the same way now that I do exist. I think kids are something you learn to like, like broccoli. I love broccoli, but if I had the choice to go back to when I was eating it out of a jar, it might not be a part of my life to this day.

He didn't want me to have kids at a young age like he did, and I'm pretty sure he wanted me to have nothing to do with the art of practicing it. Before I got my apartment, Richard lived 40 minutes away from my parents' house. It was hard to get off work at 2am and drive home instead of to his house. I wasn't allowed to spend the night at the time because I was still living under the laws of my parents, so I found a way to trick the system. I would go over to Richard's all night, not sleep and leave at 5 am to return to my bed, only to have to make the drive back to work the next morning. Technically, I wasn't sleeping anywhere. I decided my sanity and my gas tank could no longer take the four commutes a day, five days a week. I started spending the night at Richard's more often. At first, I would make up sleepovers with girlfriends or tell my dad that female co-workers were lending me one of their couches. I would stay up all night with Richard, mostly talking about what all young couples do, how much we liked each other's faces, what we were going to eat for dinner. That would have been the extent of it, if Richard had been a little bit more normal. Instead we talked about how much we liked each other's faces, what was in the "cards" for us, and more about astrological readings than anything else.

Richard was the only person I knew who could eat an entire chocolate cake and wake up the next morning with his abs more defined than ever. Sometimes, I was jealous that he was prettier than me. This was my first-time experimenting with life on my own, without my parents' consent, with a boyfriend, with a bartending artist, and with Abigail. As much as I would like to say this newfound freedom, like most young adults, had prepared me for the real world, it could not have been further from reality. It was our reality though, and if only for a few months, it made sense. My parents eventually found out it was a guy that was causing me to stay away from home, and they were not happy about it. They said that I was spending more time 'in love' than going to my place of employment, and I agreed. Love was one full-time job that was not paying my bills.

The next day, I woke up to the sound of my alarm clock buzzing, skipped my shower, put my hair into a bun, and went to work. I had only slept two hours since my last shift. My life was tiring, and my job even more so. The only thing appealing at work these days was Richard, and I didn't know how long that alone could keep me going. Serving was becoming more of a chore, and my tips were showing it. I started having to pick up extra shifts to make what I use to make in one. I had moved out of my parents' house a few months prior because they had decided to move out of state, since I was dating a guy. They never told me this was the reason why they moved but what else was I to assume. They asked me to come with them and to start building a new life consisting of going back to school. It sounded great, but I couldn't leave the place I called home and the glamorous lifestyle of a waitress just yet.

I ended up moving in with Richard and invited a permanent house guest to stay with us. My best friend and future roommate, Melanie.

I had known Melanie since middle school. She loves telling the story of how we met. She sat down next to me at the cafeteria table; one of my other good friends, Annie, had met her in math class and decided she would make a great addition to our group. Our "group" mainly consisted of everybody who didn't have a group. She fit in, but I became worried that our group was becoming too big and too noticeable. All of our friends, being the poor vultures they were, started eating her whole tray of food which consisted of soggy fries and a chicken sandwich, as soon as she sat down. I was used to this behavior and always ate most of my lunch while in line waiting to pay. That way, I wouldn't go the rest of the day starving. My friends weren't bad, just broke. I felt bad that Melanie had an empty tray sitting in front of her; she already looked like she had been starving. She probably weighed a slim ninety pounds and most of that was in her curly brown hair that sat on her head like an outdated afro. There was only one thing to do. I had saved a blue airhead from a pack of six that I had bought over my weekend just for this moment. I broke it in half and gave it to her under the table. She looked at me and smiled; her smile was kind of crooked but so was mine. I smiled back. She later told me that was one of the nicest gestures she had ever seen. I immediately felt even sorrier for this girl and decided I had to stay friends with her for the rest of her life. So, when at nineteen, she decided to move away from her parents without thinking about another place to reside first, I had to be there to help. Richard was not happy about this, but Thaun agreed to let both of us stay at his house, free of rent, if the sex was abundant! No—I kid— but he did say if the house was kept up and the occasional sink of dishes were done.

At the time, Melanie was a nursing assistant at a hospital that was thirty minutes away; her schedule was that she worked three days on and four days off. This was also the first time she had been left on her own. I would like to say we eventually grew up, but five years later we still hadn't figured shit out. Melanie and Abigail had known each other in grade school and had not seen each other since. After Melanie joined us our artistic, service industry compound, she and Abigail connected again, and I couldn't believe I had not seen the similarities in them sooner. When Melanie first met Thaun, she couldn't believe that Abigail found him attractive. I told her he would grow on her. He had an awesome personality, and I remember how much my opinion had changed since my first encounter with Thaun.

Thaun had an infectious personality; he made everything fun. A grocery store encounter with him would soon become an adventure. I loved his positive outlook on life. Eventually, more than Thaun's personality grew on Melanie and an unexpected crush developed. By the time this came around, Thaun and Abigail had been on the outs and to my surprise showed no signs another make-up session anytime soon. With Melanie's newfound freedom and grown-up responsibility, she found it a great time to make growing up official. Her plan was to seduce Thaun. This was her first attempt at anything involving true human emotion, and when she asked how she should go about it, the only thing I could think of was cookies. Chocolate chip cookies. I had made Richard chocolate chip cookies as more of an excuse to have some for myself and decided to save four.

Melanie decided to use the cookies as a way into Thaun's heart or at the very least to get upstairs and into Thaun's room. She was invited by him to come in, even though I wasn't sure he even liked cookies. After hearing the door shut behind her from the bottom of the staircase, I assumed this gesture was okay. In the morning, she told me that Thaun had ate all her cookies. This whole living situation was good for us because money wasn't all that great at this time, serving being what it always had been, a shitty job with an inconsistent sleep schedule all the while sacrificing your soul. My life needed a new direction. The sky's the limit, right?

CHAPTER SIX
CLICHÉ TITLE: MILE HIGH CLUB

I imagine serving is the same everywhere, whether in the U.S., in Europe, or while being 30,000 feet up in the air. Certainly, the view would be better from that altitude, anyway. My friend, Jane, at the time was training to be a flight attendant. It sounded like a respectable career choice and flight attendants were very important people after all. Sure, some of your duties include serving people food and drink, even worse you don't receive tips, but if somebody is being an asshole to you, you can choose to save them last in the unlikely incident the plane starts plummeting from the sky. People who ride planes have an unspoken agreement with their flight attendants. After telling my friend Abigail about the idea, she thought she should also apply to the mile-high club. I was extremely excited about my newfound passion for flying, that I never even knew I had. We both went to the interview. The airline consisted of smaller jet planes, fifty- seat passenger jets to be precise. Each flight had one attendant and no flights past the Midwest. This interview was surprisingly easy for what was supposed to be a very important job. I walked into a room in a building behind the Richmond International airport and sat at a table with five other people. The first thing they made us do was take off our shoes. You had to be a certain height so that you could reach the compartments overhead, but not too tall where they couldn't cram your ass into that Cracker Jack box they called a plane. I passed with flying colors, being of average height for most girls in their early twenties. I was feeling pretty proud of myself at this point, as if I had something to do with how my height had turned out. The next question was, "Please, raise your hand...." (Oh I so got this!)"If you have never flown before." I hesitated and looked around. Before I had time to even consider raising my hand, the instructor started laughing and said, "Good! We definitely can't have a flight attendant who has never flown before." Thank God for my naturally slow reaction times. I laughed nervously and looked at Abigail. "DUH! Who hasn't flown right?"

I hadn't flown on a plane. That's who. Was I that naive to think I didn't need experience in a plane before accepting a full-time job on one?! I got the job and I am pretty sure, based on lack of qualifications you needed for the job, the other five people in the room got the job too.

I decided to only work part-time at my current serving job while I was training to be a flight attendant. They were okay with this because I had been there for over two 'AMAZING' years. The next step of the process was to complete a six-week training course that was from six a.m. to four p.m., Monday through Friday. We had nightly homework and tests as if we were back in school. I must admit, near the end of the course, I was feeling pretty good about my decision I had made to apply for this job and the direction my life was heading. I pictured it as glamorous (think Britney Spears toxic video) strolling through the airport while people applauded us for a job well done. Hot, single pilots making our stays in unknown places feel more like home and huge paychecks.

Just then, I hear my instructor's voice say that we will have a test flight next week to PA. It will be straight there and back, just to see how a flight attendant works, and we would get to ask her questions about her everyday duties. When I got home, fear struck me. I remembered I had a fear of flying, hence why I had never flown up until that point. The idea of being 30,000 feet above anything sounded more like hell. I thought about this every day leading up to the practice flight. Even worse, I for sure thought I would blow my cover of never being on a plane when I arrived at the airport and would not know how to check in my bags. The conditions on the day of my practice flight couldn't have been worse. It was still dark out, being only 5 a.m., in the dead of winter with pouring rain. There was a huge thunderstorm playing out right in front of me through the airport windows and our flight even got delayed from its original time. Of course, I took everything as a sign and was hoping the flight got canceled all together. The flight did not get canceled, and I had limited time to rethink this job. I went to the boarding gate and entered the plane. The plane was so skinny and small. I could barely fit my head between the overhead compartments which resided on both sides of the aisle. I got to my seat and immediately strapped myself in. The takeoff wasn't as bad as I had thought it would be and almost felt like some sort of ride at an amusement park that would quickly be over. It was not nearly over. We hadn't even reached altitude yet, and my adrenaline quickly turned to fear when lightening flashed through every window on the dark plane. Rain drops hit the window so hard I thought it was hailing. It may have been hailing; I put my window shade down too quickly to find out. I suddenly had Deja vu, but why? I had never been on a plane before. Oh, yes, I'm pretty sure I saw this scene in final destination, the first one of course, way before all the deaths seemed highly ridiculous, but after recently watching 1,000 ways to die, I believe all Final Destination movies could have been based on true stories. Unfortunately, this was not a scene being shot for a movie, we weren't on a grounded flight with lighting effects. We were in the air and every five minutes; we were hitting another 'air pocket'. Ah, yes, I remember learning about these in training. Basically, every air pocket a plane hits, the plane drops altitude quickly and regains itself seconds later. I suddenly became angry with myself. Had serving been that bad? I never once had a close call while serving! All I kept thinking to myself is how pissed my dad would be if I died. I'm pretty sure I literally said, "My parents are going to kill me if I die." This seemed highly unreasonable. The next thought that crossed my mind was that I was going to die on my first day of my new job. I wondered what the news would say. To me, the news always made everything seem scary and sad, and then they finish off with a best of luck to everybody tone. I was sure that this would be no different. The news story would go as follows: FLIGHT ATTENDANTS IN TRAINING WILL NOT COMPLETE COURSE DUE TO BAD WEATHER AND EAGERNESS TO FIND A NEW DIRECTION, UNFORTUNATELY THE ONLY DIRECTION THEY SAW WAS DOWN. (News anchor has serious, but sorry smile on her face) OUR THOUGHTS AND PRAYERS GO OUT TO THEIR FAMILIES. IT LOOKS LIKE MORE BAD WEATHER IS ON THE WAY, AIRLINES CAN'T CATCH A BREAK, BACK TO YOU, DAVE! In the middle of me already envisioning making the top story on Channel 5, the captain came on announcing our descent. I couldn't wait to get back to the ground only to board minutes later and do it all over again. The thought crossed my mind to rent a car and drive back across country; I wasn't old enough to rent a car. As we were landing in PA, the sun came out; it was a completely different world than the lifetime movie I had just been acting out in my head.

I watched as the sun rose over the clouds from my plane window, it was breath taking. My fear had suddenly disappeared, and I was left with a sense of calm. Upon landing, I overheard a customer seated in front of me say, "Could the landing be any rougher?" I had to bite my tongue, two seconds away from reminding him of the ride we had just experienced and that we were lucky to have landed at all. Why waste any more time and energy on people I thought. I suddenly had an epiphany and realized it wasn't my serving job that I hated; it was the people who came to my job. It was the conceited asshole in the seat in front of me. I never finished my flight attendant career upon safely returning home. Not just because of that flight but because all the pilots were married, the airports were cluttered with angry people who didn't care to notice your uniform, and the pay was awful. There was only one thing to do...still act like I was flight attendant in order for my serving job to let me work whenever I found suitable and not having to follow any kind of schedule. I loved not having a set schedule and just being able to pick up shifts when I wanted to, the problem was I never wanted to, and my electric bill required more stability. Plus, I started to feel bad when we did a secret Santa at work the following Christmas and one of the girls gave me a mini traveling kit which would make an excellent gift for any flight attendant. I looked at my all-knowing boyfriend and then looked down in shame.

CHAPTER SEVEN
CHEATING IS LIKE GETTING FAT, IT'S GOING TO HAPPEN AT LEAST A FEW TIMES IN YOUR LIFE
(SOMETIMES BOTH HAPPEN AT THE SAME TIME)

Richard eventually got promoted to bartender, which was kind of hard to believe considering he spent most of his shifts doodling rather than with his customers. I'm sure it helped that my female manager thought he was hot. For all you know, the title of this chapter has nothing to do with what I'm about to write. So....Richard was cheating on me. Okay, I didn't know that for sure, but as soon as he got promoted, he started wanting to take relationship breaks, and though I had no proof, I'm pretty sure they were only breaks from OUR relationship. One day, all of my suspicions came true when I saw him take a bar guest who had become a regular outside. Even though we were on one of our many breaks that he made up to feel less guilty about wanting to be with somebody else, I thought it was my obligation to know what was going on. If anything, I wanted to know if that feeling inside every girl's stomach is right. I found him outside of the side door in full uniform making out with her while we were both on the clock. I started crying hysterically (what do you expect, I got note-booked by this guy!). I ran to the bathroom and no longer cared about holding it together for strangers or their food. My co-workers followed me into the bathroom to console me, but I think it was mostly to say, "We told you so." I, myself, thought I would make an excellent addition to any Nicholas Sparks film with the crying scene I was putting on at this point, on the ground, head buried in my hands, and just the right amount of mascara running down my cheeks. There was more drama between Richard and me before this, which I am choosing not to disclose here. I mainly left these other incidents out because then I would start to seem very human, and after all, I'm a server and we are not real people. Richard got in trouble and a warning for kissing on the clock from a manager that we both disliked greatly. I left in the middle of my shift, unable to pretend I cared about the temperature of someone's steak when my entire heart managed to make it into my stomach. Luckily, my usually cold-hearted manager understood and let me leave. I'm sure she had experienced something of the sort before. My relationship and my power were cut off a few days later.

I did not show up for work the next day. I would have called, if my cell phone had not been turned off, and I would have walked to the corner gas station to use the payphone, as I had done so many times before, if I had the energy. I decided not to care about anything. Later that night I would drive my irresponsible self, up to my work and explain to them that my power had been cut off, that my boyfriend had been cheating, and that I somehow thought this meant I got a "feel sorry for myself day." This had worked awhile back with another co-worker who also decided he needed a day to himself without letting anybody know. He was a young, good looking African American who somehow convinced our manager that if he could get a certain amount of signatures on a petition he had made with people convinced he should keep his job, then he should be able to keep his job. This would never work, or so I thought. I didn't even know who half the signatures on the paper were. They didn't work with us, and this didn't make sense.

She somehow thought this was a good idea and once he reached his number of signatures, which he probably received mostly from family or homeless people so that he could keep his job. Being as smart as I am, I told myself I would bring up the petition thing if anything started going south in our conversation. If anything, I would agree to make a petition with at least fifty more signatures than he had. The conversation went south immediately. I had not thought out my plan long enough. I had not considered the fact that I was a female, a female who my female manager was not attracted to, who she had not slept with. I realized my chances were slim to none. I was terminated. I didn't even want the job anymore, but somehow my conscience was telling me to try to fix this. She even offered to give me a good reference with another job. I was curious as to what she would say to my new place of employment.

"It says here that Tonya was terminated by you, but somehow she used you as a reference. Is that right?"

"Oh yes, Tonya was a great worker until she decided to get all human on me one day and I fired her. I'm sure it won't happen again. You should give her a try."

But with that, I had no job, no electricity, and no boyfriend. Things were really starting to look up. Living on my own and providing for myself was not the adulting I had been looking forward to.

The worst part of the breakup was not the fact that I was worried I wouldn't find somebody else. I was twenty-two and still marriage material. If anything, I thought I had time to improve myself, grow finer with age, and all that wine comparison bullshit.

My heart was broken, but I was told that one day that would stop working all together, so I always had that to look forward to. With no job and my three-year "open" relationship done, my best friend Melanie and I decided to move to North Carolina for a fresh start.

JUST THE TIP

CHAPTER EIGHT
THE ORIGIN OF YA'LL AND SOUTHERN HOSPITALITY

I packed up everything I owned into my white Honda CRV, and although it was packed to the top, I noticed it still wasn't much stuff between two people. Melanie was in the passenger seat and I was driving. I couldn't see behind me and the boxes completely blocked Melanie from my view. I felt like I was leaving this town alone. It was bittersweet. Richmond, Virginia didn't offer much. I mean there was Monument Park for the occasional picnics, but I never had picnics.

Why was this place on my list of things to miss? There was Belles Isle where we spent entire summers in the middle of the James River working on our tans while laying on giant boulder rocks. Hippies would play their guitars out of tune and the area was always filled with running and bicycle enthusiasts. Even I had caught myself on the occasional trail or two, out of breath, hoping to burn calories from Chanello's pizza or more importantly their chocolate chip cookies. Oh, and then there was the sidewalk cafe with their black bean nachos that instantly made any day better. Once food places started coming to mind for things to miss and not people, I realized that this move was for the best. After all, all states were required to have food.

As we went through the fan area one last time, we stopped at a light across from the main dorm rooms at VCU. The fan area was the hipster part of downtown where people were paying way too much rent for a building that was way too old. Some college kids with blonde dreads falling down their backs and seemingly stoned out of their mind, asked where we were going with all our stuff. I told them we were going to a sleepover and then drove straight to the highway. I was glad that I was going somewhere, anywhere. North Carolina was never my first choice of places to live. At first, I didn't want to give it a chance. Up until that point, Virginia was as far south as I was willing to go that didn't involve Pina Coladas and the word "vacation." The three-hour drive involved Melanie reciting a gossip magazine through a hole we made in one of the boxes that separated us, a remake of Mariah Carey's greatest hits CD, starring a duet by us on every song, and after singing "Always be my Baby" for the third time in a row in unison but completely out of key, there it was, the sign, "Welcome to North Carolina" (don't be surprised if your ass grows two sizes in the first six months). The next sign said BOJANGLES. Coincidence?! I think not. I decided not to stop at the famous chicken and biscuit joint, because at the time chicken (a dinner or lunch protein) and biscuits (a breakfast side) didn't sound appealing, especially through a drive-through window in the middle of nowhere. I don't trust fast food places that seem like business and customers are limited, even if location is just to blame. You never know how often they choose to restock or how the people working there even get there. I always look for signs that housing exists nearby. If I don't see housing within an hour before I stop driving, I shouldn't stop, and if I have to stop and eat and housing is not within up to an hour after leaving, I shouldn't have stopped.

My parents lived far from the city of Raleigh, NC, and far from a more suburban area such as Cary. The town they lived in did have more than the town I grew up in by far, but I was somehow still disappointed and depressed about my decision. This place at least had a Wal-Mart, multiple streetlights and fast food stops. I also was moving back in with my parents, along with a friend, until we got back on our feet. Back on our feet, as if we had failed miserably the six months that we were on our own. We had. I was just glad we hadn't decided to sign a year lease at our apartment. Could you imagine if we had to be grown up for a whole year? We may not have come back from a year of responsibility, and the damage would have been way too severe to repair. As much as my parents had begged me to come down in the beginning, I am pretty sure they were mad that I only agreed to it after Richard had been caught cheating, my electricity was cut off, and my food was running low. Oh, and I brought a friend, my homeless friend, my hungry friend, my non-driving, non-money having friend, my best friend.

"Can she stay? Please!?!"

I couldn't leave her in Richmond. She would've had no other choice but to move back home after being free for a year. Nobody ever left our hometown. It was in the country, and for the most part, it always stayed the same. I didn't feel like she deserved that kind of punishment, and I had no authority to assign it. Mom and Dad would have to deal. "Okay, you guys will have to pay 600 a month for rent." WHAT!!! Six hundred dollars?!! What kind of joke was this? I know this does not seem like a lot of money but tell that to the girl that just had to leave another state because she couldn't afford to eat with the lights on.

I understood making Melanie pay, but I was flesh and blood. I spent nine months in my mother's womb eating her leftover food and my own fluids, none of which was my choice, and now I had to pay to be their daughter again. It hit me that I would have to get a job. It was not quite the sitting around, watching movies, eating ice-cream, and feeling sorry for myself weeks I had counted on after losing my heart and my apartment in the same week. The only thing I felt like I hadn't lost in the past few months was weight.

Within the next few days, I went looking for a job. There wasn't much of a variety unless I wanted to start a career with Ronald McDonald. As much experience as I had with restaurants, I refused to work in fast food. I don't know why. It seemed easy and at least you were guaranteed pay, but somehow, I was addicted to working for tips. I was convincing, enthusiastic, and funny. I couldn't let my personality fade behind a screen and earpiece. I did apply to one fast food place and even got the job, but when they called to set up paperwork, I never accepted the call.

The only sit-in restaurant nearby was an American corporate chain restaurant. It wasn't a bar atmosphere where young adults would gather for drinks on the weekends. Oh, no, this place had coloring books and crayons. This was already a red flag for me, considering my prior allergy to kids. The atmosphere seemed dead or maybe it was the employees that worked there. Perhaps both. How long had they worked here, how long had they lived here? This town seemed boring and so did the people who lived there. But I hadn't even talked to anybody yet, who was I to judge? I filled out an application, praying I didn't get the job. I had an interview on the spot with a middle-aged woman with a southern twang. She looked like a smoker. Her skin was worn and her fingernails were long with a yellow tint. My grandma had the same fingernails, and she was a smoker. This manager looked around fifty years old, even though I'm pretty sure she might have been 35. I immediately got the job. So much for that. I should have felt lucky; Melanie landed a job at a local Donut shop. She started her shifts at 5 am, and even though I was looking forward to free donuts, her job sucked.

Her pay even more so. She would have made more sitting at home doing chores for my parents, but I liked that she was trying and decided I should try, too.

I asked when I could start. When any job thinks it's a good idea to wear khakis from the waist down, it's not a good sign. Dull green polo shirts and khaki shorts couldn't have described my mood better, boring, and out of place. That was now me. I looked like I fit right in, until I heard my co-workers talk. Did people really talk like this? What was this twang thing? Did people really talk this slow? Did they think this slow? I stood out; people asked me where I was from immediately. It was only a state away, but it seemed like another country. "Ya'll" was used commonly. I admit, I too, have let the word slip a few times. Even where I'm from, it was said from time to time but not like this. This "ya'll" was said in full character (Y-aa-a-lllllll) spread out over multiple syllables. The more I heard it, it became almost charming. I decided I needed to adapt to my new life and quickly adopted "ya'll" into my vocabulary.

I finally approached my first table on my first solo serving shift after training. At the table sat four older women, older than my grandma possibly.

"Hi," I began. "How are you guys doing?" They all looked at each other with almost disgust.

"There are no guys here," one of them said. I laughed. Of course, they were joking, right? They were not smiling. My smile quickly faded as well.

"I'm aware of that, it's just a saying that I am used to using." The women were offended. I was eager to move on, not knowing they took my gesture so literally and said, "Ladies, are we ready to order?"

They were picky with everything. They modified every item they ordered, and even then, the food wasn't up to par. I guess these ladies weren't the Bobby Flay they had hoped to be and the dishes they had created looked bland and unappealing. Okay, so people here who went out to eat weren't any different (not even with a southern twang). What a shame. Here I was in a brand-new place, doing the same old thing with the same picky people. My tip was almost ten percent. I blamed it on me referring to the ladies as 'you guys'. My next table was five burley men with cut-off tanks, guts practically hanging out, and dirty blue jeans. They sat down in my section and just then and only then, maybe for the first time ever, I started thinking about running into the street in front of anything moving at an extremely fast speed. As I stared out the window, I realized a car hadn't passed in over an hour. Throwing myself into the street would be pointless. With no other options, I approached the table.

"Hi, how are YA'LL doing?" I asked, having learned my lesson. Perhaps they would tip me better if they thought I was one of their own.

"Can we get the ribs?" asked one of the guys.

No "hi", no drink orders, just straight to the ribs. Why did this not surprise me?

"Sure, and can I get you something to drink?" You know, in case the unlikely incident that one of the ribs was to become launched in your throat? Perhaps you would like some manners also? Oh, just water? Okay. All five of them ordered the ribs; I tried to reply with a twang of my own and even gave them extra wet naps. They called me everything but my name, which was conveniently placed on my nametag. Hun, sweetheart, and darling were abundant throughout their stay. They were like five messy obese babies, and it was my job to keep them presentable or they would throw a fit. Was this what my life had come to? I was serving rednecks ribs who thought they were on a pet name basis with me. Even worse, they didn't tip me at all. I felt used and useless. Where was the southern hospitality that had been displayed in all the movies I had seen? Where were the southern gentlemen? These guys were neither gentle nor men. They were a breed of their own.

I mostly worked lunches after that, which were worthless if you were trying to bring home any cash at all. Sometimes, I chose to walk the six miles home in the middle of day, where North Carolina summers seemed to be the hottest. I knew I could not go on like this for long. After a few more weeks, I decided I wouldn't be called sugar one more time, for free. I never showed back up and they never called to find out why.

Before heading straight back out to look for another job that I would soon regret, I decided to see how far my very small savings would take me jobless. I took the next few weeks off and Melanie eventually had a few days off as well. We just got our tax returns and vowed on the way home that this would be the beginning of us saving for our futures, and for ten minutes, we both believed it. We went on my parents' patio to enjoy the beautiful weather North Carolina seems to offer most of the year, completely ignoring the fact that it was my parents' patio, meaning we were completely incapable of living on our own at this point of our lives.

That is when I got a phone call from our friend, Annie. Annie was one of our best friends all through school, starting from the 5th grade. Annie was 5'6" with shoulder-length red—sometimes orange— hair before she started dying it. She had a thicker build up top and nice legs. Her eyelashes were one of her best features. They were incredibly long and with mascara looked like any drag queen's dream show lashes. She was also a habitual liar. We all knew this, but we didn't mind. She was entertaining and kept us laughing non-stop and that outweighed the lies.

Annie once told me right after high school that her mom had passed away. I felt really bad, but Annie never got along with her mom for the most part anyway. But that's no excuse, a person dying, especially your best friend's mother, is a reason to mourn. She was so nonchalant about it that I just wrote it off as her way of dealing with what I imagined would be very hard to deal with. Fast forward to a few months later, Annie and I are having another conversation, mostly catching up with each other on the phone about how our lives did not go anywhere close to the directions that we saw them taking, when she said, "My mom is back on drugs."

Ummmmmmmmmmmmmmmmmmmmmmmmmmmmmmmmmm.

"YOUR MOM?"

"Yes, can you believe that, after everything we have been through with her?"

"Um, no. I can't believe that your mom is back on drugs, but I imagine coming back from the dead would make anybody turn to drugs."

Annie then replied with, "What are you talking about? My mom is not dead." I then reminded Annie of our previous conversation, the one where we were mourning her mom's death and I was asking her about funeral arrangements. She then came up with a story of how she thought her mom had died because her mother's roommate, who was also on drugs, had called and told Annie that her mom had died in hopes to get her to come over and see her mom who had apparently passed away but not really. I admired her quick train of thought. So, you can imagine how surprised Melanie and I were to be receiving another phone call from her after a few years hiatus again. I looked at Melanie before answering and said, "If she tells me her mom has died one more time, I may lose my shit."

This time, however, she simply started the conversation with, "Hey, how are you?"

"I'm great," I said, "if you consider great living back at your parents' house with your best friend from middle school." (Honestly at times, it was great.) She then went on to tell me she had married a military guy a year earlier and was living an hour from me in North Carolina on a military base.

"Oh, that's great! The marriage and the fact that we may be able to see each other!"

She said she would love to see Melanie and me, and I opted to drive to meet up with her that night. I must admit, I was pretty excited to see Annie; she was never boring and always fun. Somebody who would follow through with any one of my spontaneous ideas, even when everybody else would opt for safer activities. She would do anything and never cared what people thought, which I thought were admirable qualities to have in a friend. I told Melanie that she was going to meet up with us tonight and go out downtown.

Later on that night, when Annie met up with us, we asked her questions about her husband and told her we were shock we didn't hear the news sooner, thinking we would at least be invited to the wedding.

"There was no wedding; we just went to the courthouse."

Well, that sounded romantic. She then told us that they were going through a divorce, but not yet legally separated. I didn't know whether I should believe that she was married or only after a year already getting a divorce, but I had no reason not to. After all, she hadn't lied to me since she told me her mother died, and who hasn't told a few white lies before? After a few drinks, she told us she had gotten a tattoo of herself on her thigh for her friend's tattoo expo. We asked her to see it.

"Well, here's the thing, it's really good artwork but it's me... sucking a...." I will let you fill in the rest. I was in shock, what stable person lets this happen! I immediately wrote it off as her lying yet again, trying to get another reaction out of us. She didn't show us. I told her our reason for going out tonight should be to celebrate her divorce and new beginnings. We picked Soco limes as a shot of choice for every bar we went to that night and decided we were all going to get wasted in celebration of another marriage not lasting in society. We got a hotel room for the night, right in the middle of downtown, so that we wouldn't have to drink and drive. Our night started with food and drinks and shots and more shots and more shots, then some guys buying us shots, and then karaoke. We were horrible, and I lip-synced through most of it.

As the night was ending, we were trying to walk back to our hotel when two guys that we had met earlier stopped to say hi. They were driving a nice black truck with all tinted windows and asked if we would like a ride. I was a little skeptical of getting in a fully tinted truck with two guys we barely knew, but drunk doesn't know skeptical, so it passed for a good decision. Melanie, Annie, and I hopped in the car with our potential kidnappers and thankfully made it back to our hotel room. I got out as quickly as possible when the guys asked if they could come up. My immediate answer was, "No."

"Sure," Annie said, contradicting me.

"ANNIE!!!" The whole way up, I was thinking how uncomfortable this situation had suddenly become. All I wanted to do was shove my face full of horrible food and fall asleep just to look forward to waking up and feeling like shit. Ah, the perks of drinking. When we finally got in the room, Annie hopped in one of the beds and tried to go to sleep. Is she serious right now? She invited two unattractive strangers up to our room and then goes to sleep, leaving Melanie and I with two guys expecting to be entertained. I wasn't feeling it at all. Melanie somehow thought giving one of the guys a massage was a good idea. She picked the more attractive one. The other friend who was a lot older and more overweight then asked me if I wanted one. I didn't.

I tried to go to sleep, only to awake up later to find both guys in our bed in their underwear and spooning me. Four people in a queen bed. I felt nauseous and was just about to go to the bathroom when I saw Annie get up to go in first who was sharing a bed to herself in a hotel room I paid for with our wonderful savings we had started. I went to the bathroom and knocked on the door and told her I was uncomfortable with the situation. She cut me off in the middle of my sentence and said we must get them to leave now. I agreed. I didn't ask questions as to why. I woke them up. It was early morning and I told them we had to leave the room and get ready for work. They got up, groggy, and started to put their clothes on. We rushed them out after exchanging numbers that they were sure we were never going to use. At least they were smart. As soon as they left, Annie ran to lock the door and started laughing. I told her I was pissed at her display last night when she said she was sorry but that she wasn't really sleeping.

She was faking it until they fell asleep so she could steal the money in their wallet.

"WHAT!?"

Not ten minutes later, we got a call from the guys saying that they were sure they were missing money and must've left it in our room and were coming back up to get it. We threw on our clothes as quickly as possible and ran down the exit stairs to go look for our cars that we had left at the bar before we started drinking. We looked like shit and I was hungover.

"Annie, why would you even think to steal their money and more importantly how much is it?"

"I wanted to pay you back for last night, buying most of our drinks and stuff, and it was around two hundred dollars."

As bad as it sounds, that pretty much paid for our entire night and hotel so I broke even with a good time, which never happens when you go out drinking, never. Annie was always like that. Shady, ballsy, and one of my good friends. After we found our car, we went home to shower and I asked Annie about her tattoo one more time. She refused to show us. I wondered why she would lie about something so stupid. Melanie must have been thinking the same thing. She ran up to Annie after her shower and pulled off her towel. Annie screamed! There it was. Just as she had described it. A beautiful, permanent portrait of her face, in perfect detail, with a guy's penis beside her mouth. I couldn't believe it. She wasn't lying. It was on her upper leg, around her thigh. There was no way she could ever wear a bathing suit without it being seen again. She told us she was thinking about getting the penis covered up with something like a flower. Perfect, I thought. A portrait of her eating a flower.

Annie ended up staying in North Carolina until her divorce was almost final. He was always at work and she never worked. I only met him once and it was after coming to pick Annie up after they had gotten in a huge fight outside their military housing apartment. When I pulled up, I understood exactly why they were fighting. This place was horrible. The only places I passed on the way there were pawn shops, used car lots, and gun stores. Every single one of these places was the same, with thick black bars on the windows seeming to be the exterior decoration of choice. When I pulled up to their driveway, waiting for her to jump through the window telling me to book it, I had time to notice most of her neighbors were on the porch enjoying the show. Every single porch had a young girl on it, probably younger than me, all carrying babies. I don't know if it was because the area was so poor or because the housing this base provided offered no yards or trees, but I all of a sudden felt sorry for every girl there. I was never a girl that had a dream of getting knocked up by some military hotshot and be a stay at home mom while my husband was gone more than half the year.

Just then I heard glass break. "What the fuck?"

Annie came to my car crying and we left. "What were you guys fighting about?" I asked. Besides the obvious, I thought.

"He's cheating on me. I knew he was from the beginning. He told me he never loved me."

"I'm glad you're getting a divorce then."

Annie's sadness only last for an hour tops before she started plotting her revenge. Later, he was going to a friend's house to spend the night, so we went back with Melanie's house. As soon as we got there, Annie started looking for stuff to pawn, specifically his stuff to pawn. She only had some lamps, a nice vacuum that I told her she should keep, and his military guns, which she was not allowed to touch. This coming from her ex-fiancé and the government. We woke up the next day and I told her we should go to the beach for the day to keep her mind off things. He had left their brand-new Nissan in the driveway; his "friend" must have given him a ride. This was perfect! My car was such a piece of shit, and I always questioned if I would come back from any of my spontaneous need-to-escape-from-life trips. You would be surprised to hear that they never work out the way I intend for them to.

We got in his car and starting driving. Melanie was supposed to work that night, but we told her she should call out. She started worrying about losing her amazing cocktailing job at the place that I had already been fired from twice. So, I did what any good friend would do. I lied.

"Fine. We will be back before you need to go to work. Don't worry about it." Melanie sat back in her seat, comforted by the fact that she was still employed. I texted Annie to tell her to keep driving south to South Carolina. After a while and after passing "Welcome to another fucking state???" as Melanie liked to put it, I was pretty sure Melanie realized that working tonight was not in the cards for her. We stopped in Folly Beach, SC right outside of Charleston. It was a very cool beach town, most of which had been damaged by a few tropical storms. We stayed on the beach all day and went to a beach bar at night where we pretty much spent the last of the money we had saved for our bright new future. I was looking at it. My future. A fishbowl frozen margarita. It all makes sense now.

After sharing an appetizer to make sure we had enough gas money to get home, we walked around the beach one more time, none of us willing to be the first to say it was time to return to reality, which none of us wanted to be real. I texted Annie again so that Melanie was not apart of our conversation and said I had enough to get to Florida. Maybe then we could see my ex and he could help us get the money to get back. I know what you are thinking, why would my ex give me money? That is not what you were thinking? Annie wrote back and said she was unsure of my idea and was worried we would get stuck, not to mention her ex-husband would soon find his car to be missing. I told her it was our last chance for all three of us to be together for a while. By the way, we kept Melanie out of this conversation entirely.

We started heading back on the road and Melanie lay down to fall asleep in the back seat. By the time, she woke up we were in Georgia. "Where are we?" Melanie asked. "We are almost home." This was a lie. We were going south. "What are you guys doing?! I have to work tomorrow!"

"Well, we are going to Florida, so you are going to have to call in one more time. Just say you have been kidnapped and then you won't feel so bad about lying."

We finally made it to Florida by 10 a.m. I only knew my ex, Richard there and had only been there once to visit him after he had sent me a text saying that we should no longer see each other. He had no idea I was coming. We hadn't talked since the breakup which had been the year prior. So here we were with no address, no phone number, and no money. My plan is going exactly as planned. I could tell Annie and Melanie were getting pissed at me and I understood why, but there was nothing we could do about it now. I had remembered his house being near a Busch Gardens. After asking somebody where the Busch Gardens were, we started taking roads that I thought looked familiar to me. We then passed the school where he said his brother attended last time I was here. I could tell we were getting close. Every neighborhood was gated and all looked the same. I remembered pink condos being in front of his complex when we went on a bike ride last summer and there they were. We pulled into what I remembered being his complex to find that the gate could only be opened if you were buzzed in. There was no way to get in, and the metal fence was too high to jump over and too slick to climb. Finally, a car was coming out and we book our asses through the wrong entrance.

The look on Richard's face when he opened the door was priceless. He immediately closed the door but then opened it again. Thank God. We were all so tired.

"Are you serious right now?" he asked me.

His face looked as if he had seen a ghost. "I know its last-minute notice, but can we nap here? And then we promise we will leave."

Luckily, we had always been better friends than lovers, and he let us stay for the whole day and whole night. After sleeping for a few hours, he told us he had to go run some errands and led us in the direction of the closest beach. The beach there was beautiful. The sand was as white as snow, and the water was completely clear. Annie wore a skirt in the water to cover up the tattoo. She told us she knew she looked retarded swimming in a skirt but that the tattoo probably looked more stupid. I agreed. Melanie was on the sand walking back and forth on the phone. She came back smiling.

"Well? Do you still have your job?" I sarcastically asked her.

"Yup. I'm in bed sick."

We stayed at the beach all day and then went back to Richard's place. The plan was to go out downtown, but we were all so tired that we stayed in and watched movies and ordered Sonic takeout. I'm sure he loved our company.

When we woke up the next day, the no money problem suddenly came creeping back up on us. Annie tried to call her dad and ex-husband for a loan. That didn't go over so well with either one of them since apparently, she owed them both a lot of money. I couldn't call my parents because of the fact that they would literally kill me. Melanie had nobody to call. I went through my phone looking for anybody I was willing to lose a friendship over, only one number came up.

"Hey, remember the guys from the hotel? Well, they told us they had a lot of money, remember?"

The night we had met them, all they talked about what how much money they had, how money wasn't a problem for them (hence Annie thinking to grab their wallets, also, I realize that act was not okay).

"You have got to be kidding me, I'm not calling them! I stole money from them, remember?" said Annie.

Well, I didn't see any other options, so it's worth a try! Annie finally gave in after realizing we were truly stuck in Florida. She called them and to all of our surprise, one of them answered. She explained who she was and denied that she ever took any of their money. She then started crying on the phone saying her car broke down and she couldn't get in touch with anybody she knew. She offered to pay him back when she got back. She hung up the phone. I knew her award-winning crying scene had not worked like we had hoped.

"We have to go to Walmart."

"Why?!" I asked.

"He is sending us 400 dollars through a money order."

"Are you serious? What did you promise him, endless sundaes and blowjobs?" She told us that he said he would just like to see us again and hang out when we got back in town but was pretty sure he would never hear from us again. Like I said, a very smart guy. I couldn't believe a complete stranger sent us money to get home. It made me question the people that were actually close to me, and I decided I needed to make more friends with more money.

JUST THE TIP

.

CHAPTER NINE
RUMPLE MINZE AND MIDGETS DANCED IN MY HEAD

It could not have been worse or more perfect timing. An acquaintance from high school named Jake had just moved to Colorado from my hometown, and thanks to social networking sites, he had the tools to contact me about having the same anxiety that I was also experiencing due to moving to a new place. In high school, I barely knew Jake, but I had a crush on him the size of Texas. After years of not talking, we found ourselves contacting each other to talk about how we both moved away from the town we knew so well and how depressing but exciting a new place could be. My place was the depressing one, his was exciting.

Jake let me know that the place he was now living in had a guy to girl ratio of 10:1. I instantly thought, what lucky bitches. After talking for a few days, not even a full day if we are considering hours or minutes, he did what any acquaintance does, he invited me to come visit him in Colorado, I assumed only to better help the guy-to-girl ratio he was having difficulties with. The first thought to cross my mind of many was, of course I should fly across country with no job, no money, and a fear of flying that was way too large to carry on any plane. This sounded like an awful idea until he offered to pay for my flight and stay. I relayed to him that I only had ten dollars in my pocket in case there was any getting out of this. I turned around to ask Melanie what she was thought of this bizarre idea to find her unzipping my suitcase, holding up outfits with thumbs up or down. She demanded I go. She was there throughout high school, and she experienced the same crush I once had for Jake. I asked her if she would go if she was offered and she replied with, "Yes! You are so lucky!"

She later told me, "I don't know how you got on that plane; I would have never done that." This whole idea seemed crazy. A guy that I only knew from the hallways of high school invites me to come visit him across the country where I would soon become the 2 in the 10:2 ratio of guys to girls. This would leave my friend who just moved in with my parents to fend for herself for ten days. My parents had left a few days prior to drive to Chicago to visit my mom's parents for Thanksgiving. They wanted me to watch the house and, more importantly, my homeless friend. After all was thought through, this was an opportunity not to be missed. I only hoped he had not changed much from high school in the way that he started murdering young girls he was once familiar with for fun. I took the chance and boarded the plane. This was the contraption that I had sworn off after to my near-death experience while training to be a flight attendant.

Ah yes, hello, old friend. My anxiety started causing me to breathe heavily, and I had managed to convince myself that the flow of oxygen was limited. Just then, a flight attendant came to the back of the plane and said that she needed my seat. Great. Not even two minutes into my flight, I was unwelcome. She told me I could move up front where I had three seats to myself. The flight was at night and four hours long. The dark didn't leave much scenery for me to see outside, so I decided to take advantage of my three seats, two of which I didn't pay for and lie down completely. This was the furthest west I had been up until this point in my life, and I slept the entire way. It felt like I had been sleeping forever when I woke up in a panic. Surely, I had missed my stop. What if I had forgotten to get off the plane, would they have woken me? Why was it taking so long? I quickly grabbed a flight attendant and asked her what time it was. Forgetting about the four-hour time difference, my face turned to terror. Had I been on this plane for eight hours? Just then, I started to think how disgusting it was for me to lay my head down in a seat that probably touched a million asses for potentially up to eight hours. "How much longer?!" I asked.

She told me we would start our descent at any time now. She could probably see the look of relief on my face. (Of course, they let people sleep on the plane and catch the next one home without notifying them) I landed safely at the airport and didn't want to think about boarding anytime soon.

Jake was there, waiting to pick me up. He looked the same as before with a little more facial hair and still cute. However, that was not my reason for being there. I was not a mail-ordered date, although I was technically paid for. Oh my God, did this make me a prostitute?! Of course not. Prostitutes get rooms paid for, not flights. I was so nervous about the whole situation that I had forgotten what my luggage had looked like. They all started looking the same and the suitcase was never mine to begin with. The suitcase was Melanie's, and I hadn't paid much attention to it leading up to this moment. After a while, we started checking names on any suitcase that resembled mine, when it suddenly hit me that I had watched my suitcase go around at least eight times. He seemed annoyed; he must have counted with me. It was dark outside, and he lived an hour from the airport. I thought the ride would be awkward but we both did a great job at filling in the silences with the art of conversation. My mood was lifted instantly.

When we arrived, I met his roommate Lindsey. Lindsey was tall with an athletic build. She had short brown hair and seemed very easy going. I wondered if she, too, had thought it was weird that I flew across the country to see some guy I had no romantic past or present with. Maybe she didn't know. We went to bed early, and I woke up to completely new scenery that I had missed out on during the previous night's drive home. The views from the window that went from the floor to the ceiling were breathtaking. The mountains were covered with snow and placed right outside my window. Up until this point, I had never seen real snowcapped mountains and was convinced now that the mountains at home were just tree covered hills. Jake had to go to work, and I was left by myself. I walked through the condo, watched TV, and took a shower. I was hungry and bored. When he finally came home, he said he was getting sick and the change of altitude was to blame. I didn't want to stay in all night or watch another Anthony Bourdain episode that had turned into a marathon while Jake was at work. Lindsey asked me if I wanted to join her at the local bars and go see a guy, she was interested in who bartended at one of them. I asked Jake if he would care but then told Lindsey I was broke. They both told me not to worry about it. The guy-girl ratio that I had mentioned earlier somehow meant I didn't need money to go out, having female reproductive organs and all. She insisted and we went out.

The first bar we went to was where she was currently employed at. I was greeted with shots of Rumple Minze, and this started my love for thick, mint cough syrup that had the ability to get me drunk. It also caused a warming sensation instantly that was good for the extremely cold weather. A few free shots later, she had already been proven right. The next bar we went into, we were swarmed with at least four guys upon entering. I looked around and the only other girl in sight was a bartender. Luckily, she had a lot of wood between her and the freakishly uneven ratio of males. Somewhere between Rumple Minze and a stale Bud Lite taste, I heard the word midget being tossed around in conversations throughout the night. As I got more intoxicated, the midget conversations became more abundant. I must have asked at least ten times what people were talking about, but in my drunken blur, I never listened long enough to find out the answer.

We then finally made our way to the bar where Lindsey's friend Paul worked. I'm pretty sure my cut off point was left back at the first bar, but this was our whole point of being out and decided I should stay strong. What kind of wing woman would I be if I bailed now? I excused myself upon entering his bar, which was also Jake's place of employment and decided the only way I was going to be able to drink was if I got rid of everything else I had before. I stumbled into a stall after trying to figure out why the floor was slanted and how I wasn't slanting with it but in the opposite direction of it. When I finally sat my now two-pounds-lighter body on a bar stool, Paul started us a bar tab that felt endless. Had we forgotten to tell him that we were low on funds? As the night neared to an end and it came time to pay, he informed us that our drinks had been sporadically rationed out on these guys' tabs across the bar that were too wasted to notice.

I always had said I wanted to start bartending when I had turned twenty-one. It was a position of respect in the restaurant and bar industry if only that it consisted of making more money and controlling people's liquor. People were always wary of how much liquor or how little bartenders would pour them, not knowing that asking the bartender to make a drink strong would taste exactly the same unless they were willing to pay for a double. I never went out of my comfort zone of cocktailing to apply to bartend up until this point, even though I thought I would make a great bartender. Maybe I was just meant to be a people server. If it was good enough for Jesus to get satisfaction in serving others, then it had to be good enough for me. I wish that was the case. I'm sure Jesus had a lot more patience than me and was ultimately more forgiving.

We waited for our new bartender, con-artist friend to get off work because of Lindsey's extensive crush on him. We then walked out onto a cobblestone walkway that led through the town. Everything was lit up in white Christmas lights. The town looked like something out of a movie, and though it was only Thanksgiving, snow covered everything. Then, standing there, in the middle of what looked like a snow globe was the topic of our conversations all night. The conversations, which had made no sense to me until right now. There was a little person standing by a roundabout with a clipboard. I, in my drunken stupor screamed out, "Oh my God! There is a midget! All night we were talking about midgets and now here one was!" I couldn't control my happiness. I had been the first one to figure this whole thing out. It wasn't a coincidence. They had been talking about midgets all night because a midget was the person who made sure you had a cab ride home after you left the bar. All of the people I was with had lived through this experience before on multiple nights, I am sure.

He looked almost elf like in this Christmas town. I was in a real-life postcard and it took my all not to ask him for a picture. Right then, black and white Hummers lined the entire roundabout. I had never ridden in a Hummer and couldn't believe this was my cab ride home. Without thinking, I blurted out, "Did a midget just put us in a Hummer?" I was sure one of my weirdest dreams was playing out right in front of me, and I couldn't help but smile all the way home. My smile quickly faded after getting home and having to run straight to the bathroom. The floor no longer seemed stable. I spent the night on the bathroom floor holding onto the toilet for dear life. I was awakened when Jake needed to get ready for work and chose to walk over my body to get in the shower. I felt like shit and every day I was there it seemed like Jake was getting sicker, or perhaps he just didn't want me there. It didn't really bother me. If he wanted to pay for me to come out and play with his roommate for ten days, then so be it. I spent most of the days with Lindsey and her friends including Thanksgiving, which Jake shortly joined us for. I pretty much spent the first night with Jake, the next few with Lindsey, one random encounter with a friend of a friend, some more Lindsey, and then Jake who would have to take me to the airport in the morning, which was more than an hour away. Soon it would be time to give up flasks of Rumple Minze and return home where no midgets would be waiting for me to make sure I got safely into a hummer ever again.

I decided as soon I got home that I would need to tell my parents that I quit my job, due to the lack of rent money I would not be providing. I didn't want to serve anymore; I needed to think of something else. So what to do when you have returned home from a ten-day vacation where you saw landscapes you thought only existed on green screen, just to remember you are jobless and you spent your last twenty dollars on a cab ride home from the airport? Just then, Melanie informs me, as soon as I walk through the door, that she is in love with somebody who she has never met, who lives in Connecticut all because she saw a commercial offering a free weekend on an internet dating site. I sulked. I was depressed, and I was going through ice-cream like it was water. I needed to get away, even if it was just for a quiet night out. This would be hard especially when, on top of everything, my car decided to make a second home at the auto shop.

I needed a change. And fast.

CHAPTER TEN
JACK ASSES

This would take me convincing my brother to take me and my equally pathetic friend out with him. I decided food bribes work the best with him, due to the fact that he hates spending his money on anything that maintains his survival. We decided to venture out to a more populated town about thirty minutes away. It was nice. It seemed more upper class, and from what I could see, most of the people looked normal with most of their teeth intact. We decided to go to this bar that was named after a donkey. A huge projection screen on their patio had caught our eye from across the parking lot. We went in and sat down. We were greeted by a guy who resembled Tracy Morgan but was taller. His shirt said something cute like, "Poke me and I'll poke back", mocking Facebook. We all thought it was funny and decided to comment on it as if we weren't customer 10,000 to say something "clever" about it. He rolled his eyes and asked us what we wanted to eat. He was kind of rude but funny so that you couldn't tell if he was being serious or not. We looked like three young kids with no money and we all ordered burgers. The atmosphere was vibrant, much different from the bar I had just quit. There were at least twenty flat screen TVs lining the bar and walls. It looked like a fun place to work.

I started to think that maybe I didn't need to quit serving, just get out of the dead-end town I had been brought to. I asked for two applications, one for me and one for Melanie. I could tell our server didn't think much of it, but I knew we would soon be co-workers. For a depressed broke girl who lived with her parents, I still had my confidence. We left a good tip, just to shock the hell out of him. Within the next two days, I went back up to the bar with my application and unmotivated roommate. I asked to speak to a manager. A younger, good-looking, high-energy guy in his later 20s to early 30s approached us. He was the bar manager and seemed overly positive and nice. He seemed interested in what we had to say and why we wanted to work there. Next, was a young lady, not as vibrant but still polite who asked very straight to the point questions without seeming to care about our answers. At this point, I was thinking we had about a 50/50 chance of getting this job. Then, it was time to meet the owner. This place seemed harder to get into than an American idol audition in front of the actual judges. The owner was very tall, older, with white hair and white strands protruding from his chin resembling a beard. He looked mountain man like, not how I would expect an owner of a restaurant to look. Perhaps an owner of a dog was more appropriate. I wondered if he had dogs, but I never asked. He was also very straight forward with his questions but seemed like he was trying to trip me up on my own answers. I didn't like this guy from the beginning but put on a smile and charmed it up. I needed a job. The only thing that we had in common was that we had both put in time at a nationwide corporate chain restaurant, which I didn't find reason enough to get a liking for each other. He was very cocky without looking the part, and I could tell I was in the presence of somebody who "knew everything." My opinion would never be valid. I was used to corporate assholes and decided this couldn't be any worse than what had already been dealt my way. After what seemed like thirty minutes with me one on one, and without even two full sentences to Melanie in her interview, he asked if we were a package deal. After nodding our heads yes, he hired us both.

Melanie had lied on her application and said she had served before, but she hadn't. I told her to lie. Up until that point, the only service she had provided to the general public was bagging their groceries or inserting catheters as a nursing assistant. Both of which I thought were very helpful services and serving was something she would learn easily. The first few days of training were classroom stuff. We sat there while listening to our floor manager, who was younger than us, give us information on what was expected from us at this job. She was only nineteen, but she acted older. It was still weird and degrading. All we really did in classroom was taste all the different food items that were offered on the menu, most of which were prepared half on the oven top and the other half in the microwave. After the second day, I learned to bring an appetite because trying ten dishes a night on top of my daytime ice-cream addiction was not helping my waistline. After all this, she gave us a spandex shirt and skirt to wear. At least it was all black, I thought. We all got to pick out three different shirts with funny sayings on them that everybody else was wearing as well and to make things worse it came as a long v neck sleeveless muscle shirt. The cut was very unappealing. We were told we could wear tank tops underneath; which Melanie chose to do more often than not. I didn't understand why she was trying to cover up her barely-there A cups. I, on the other hand, chose to not wear a tank top underneath, mostly because the shirt was already thick and uncomfortable and stuck to my body like a glove. I felt like nothing else was going to fit under it, other than a bra. I decided I would have to give up eating in general on days I had to work and wondered if five days without eating every week would eventually kill me. This outfit or job hardly seemed worth dying over; they would have to take me, with love handles and all. Melanie and I both started off in the dining room. The dining room was very "family like". All the tables had brown paper on them used as tablecloths and a cup of crayons. WAIT! WAIT! WAIT! I had obviously forgotten to tell them about my condition. I wasn't supposed to be within twenty feet of crayons due to the crowd they were likely to draw in. One of the cool parts about working in the dining room was that we all had to learn how to write our names upside down on the table. This was cool for about five minutes out of the whole two years that I worked here. Every table liked to try and guess what you were writing before you finished like a game, even though as soon as they found out it was my name, they never chose to use it when asking me for things and lost interest quickly.

Some would ask how long it took for me to master writing my name upside down. Um, about five minutes. Was this a serious question? I admit I can count my talents on one hand, but did I not come off as completely capable of writing my own name upside down? It made me sad when I started to think this could be one of the only skills I possessed. This would go on a future resume as follows: Can write my own name upside down in record time. Sad. (write name upside down) Sorry, I had the urge to see if I could still do it. A few days into my new job, I got the hang of things as with most of my other serving jobs. The only difference between one serving job and another is the workload, management, and sometimes computer programs, but the basic layout is always the same. So, to the say the least, I caught on very quickly, this not being my first time around and all.

My first week, I didn't see or speak much to Melanie, even though we both worked the same shifts since we shared the same ride. The same ride that neither of us owned, the same ride meaning my younger brother. For twenty-three, I was sure this is what rock bottom looked like. The reason for me not seeing Melanie much at work was because she was weeded through most of her shift, confused for the other half, and had no time to multi-task as she put it. Multi-tasking meaning talking and working at the same time which was the one quality if anything else that all servers were supposed to possess. I would walk by her section periodically to check up on her and to see if she needed help. I didn't want our boss to find out that we had forged her waitressing experience, and both have to be called out on fraud. Her section was a disaster; it looked like the lifeboats that had been left after the final piece of the Titanic had sunk. They looked hungry and thirsty, very thirsty. I'm pretty sure a few customers were too thirsty to call out when I walked by and instead mouthed the word HELP in silence. I tried to give people a quick smile as to say everything was going to be okay. They would give me a look back that said, what are you fucking smiling about? I haven't had a refill in about an hour and am pretty sure my waitress never put in my food order. I looked for Melanie to see if there was a reason why she was boycotting her tables. I saw her at the bar trying to figure out how to put five tables refills on a single tray at once. I decided to grab a pitcher of water and help her out, but no matter what section she had in those first few weeks, her tables would be waterless. I asked her why she never would refill her tables' drinks and told her that was one of the main factors considered when customers were deciding to leave a tip, and she would reply that she was too busy. Too busy to serve your tables? I tried to remind her that this is how she was going to make her money and that no refills usually meant no tips. I expected this from a rookie server, but this was no rookie according to her application, and I decided not to care if she was found out to be a fraud or a liar. I, after all, didn't lie on my application, and although they hired us as a package, certainly they wouldn't fire us as one too. Melanie eventually got better with the serving; she was an overly nice person anyways, and it worked well with having to please people all the time. She soon adopted the art of kissing ass for tips. I felt bad that I had brought her into my world. Once you get into serving, it's a love/hate relationship that is very hard to get out of, and you can never figure out which side is winning.

A few weeks in when I thought Melanie had this serving thing under control, she came running into the kitchen in a panic. She looked very concerned and instantly checked the temperatures of the soup, "My table is mad that their soup is cold!" I didn't see this to be a huge problem, luckily for us, our kitchen had the gourmet skills of a teenager and microwaves lined the back line, but Melanie looked like a kid who just found out Santa Claus wasn't real. She looked disappointed, confused, and furious, all over soup. I told her to warm it up and move on with her life. I went on to finish my salad that I was making. She then said in a loud tone, "Are you fucking kidding me?? These people are mad that their soup is cold, and when I told them I would warm it up, they acted completely pissed at me. I didn't cook their soup, and I don't care if their soup is cold. I had to deal with pissed people who were dying in the hospital, compared to that, this is just unacceptable." I was used to this kind of behavior from people, and it almost amused me that, after all these years of me telling her of my serving woes, she finally understood. If she thought the soup was a rough experience, she was in for a very rude awakening. As for me, I was in for a very early awakening for my double the next day.

I started my dreadful lunch shift (all lunch shifts are dreadful). I had a few tables during the day, nothing great. After I bought myself lunch and refilled my gas tank, I was sure I was going to barely break even. It was now time for my dinner shift. Dinner shifts always made more money, and most restaurants required you to work a few morning shifts to assure you got the night ones. I approached my first table of the night, a young couple. I hated waiting on young couples, mostly because they always seemed bothered by my presence, and I also felt like most of the female counterparts of the couple thought I was trying to steal their man, or boy. Just because I was a waitress who wore a D cup bra, did not mean I was on the prowl to go cougar hunting. I know twenty-three is hardly old enough to be considered a cougar, but when we're talking about teenagers here, it's comparable. Sometimes, I would smile and talk more to the guy if the girl seemed catty enough, just to get on her nerves. This only lasted until about the fifth time I saw a girlfriend take the check book from her boyfriend's hands and fill in my not so amusing tip. They paved way for a new rule that I always use now out of respect. I always make sure that I make eye contact with the girlfriends equally, if not more than the boyfriend. Sometimes you get cool couples who don't stereotype you into a waitressing whore which is cool. Some may even joke with you and not get jealous if you happen to laugh at their partner's jokes. My first young couple was fine. They didn't seem to want to be bothered like I expected, but I didn't feel like being bothered much myself either. I was just glad that we were on the same page. They made out most of the time, probably before their moms were expected to pick them up, and they left me an 18 percent tip because they had no idea how valuable their mom's money was. The next table I received was an older couple, probably in their mid to late 40's. I approached the table like I always do. They sat on the same side. I always think waiters and waitresses get annoyed with this because it left the other seat empty and never left enough elbow room to eat. I wanted to be annoyed too but sometimes, when the guy is right, I am that annoying counterpart of a couple who wants to sit on the same side of the booth. I did my spiel like I always do, and they gave me their food order. I dropped off their food. The lady at the table was very quiet with me which I just wrote off as her being a snooty bitch. At the end of their meal, they called my manager over. I didn't think anything was wrong and assumed they had complaints about their food or the fact that the woman's nose was permanently stuck in an up position. Only one of these complaints could be managed by a manager. Nothing had gone too terribly wrong. Perhaps they were complimenting me and my waitressing skills. How nice I thought. My manager called me into the hallway as my table was leaving and as I was waiting to hear her say what a good job I did I was rudely interrupted with "Your boobs offended that lady". "My what? My boobs?" You mean the two, large circular shapes of fat coming from my body that I have no control over, even with a double supported sports bra? "Yes, the lady said she noticed her husband would not stop looking at you and felt you shouldn't have been wearing such a low-cut shirt." "If her husband is looking at me and not her, that hardly seemed like my problem." I suggested that she should maybe not wear turtlenecks because they are very unflattering on almost everybody. Thinking my manager would find this funny because clearly the woman who felt the need to tell my manager my boobs were too big was obviously insane. My manager did not think I was funny and presented me with a high-necked large t-shirt. It was large in all the wrong places. She told me she thought I should wear this shirt while serving in the dining room because of the high family volume (Damn families again). The shirt looked nothing like what everybody else was wearing, and I didn't think it was fair for me to change my uniform, just because I had more than collarbone where the V-neck of my uniform resides. I refused to wear the shirt. So I was in the bathroom, putting on this hideous piece of fabric they made into a shirt, when I suddenly broke into tears. This was clearly discrimination! I or my boobs didn't do anything to anybody, at least not that night. My bosses decided I was perhaps more suitable for bar shifts as a cocktail waitress, and I agreed. My boobs and I have never had a problem with bars or people that went to bars. I hated waiting on kids and families anyways. Nothing against families, after all I have one, which I happen to like and on occasion go out to eat with but that is beside the point.

Working in the bar at this place was something people wanted to do. It was something you usually had to work for and put in time for, but I had my boobs, a forty-year-old bitter woman, and her pervert husband to thank for me being there. I had wanted to work in the bar area as soon as I had stepped foot into this establishment back when Melanie, my brother, and I all indulged in burgers. The bar was very high energy and high volume. The dining room was dead and depressing. That lady unknowingly gave me a recommendation for a promotion, and I made a note to myself to somehow personally thank her one day. This is my notice of thanks. This would start my career as a cocktail waitress. It was a whole other ball game. It was going from amateur to pro, and the money was there to back it up. With cocktailing, you have to have a certain kind of personality. Getting hit on by a hundred drunk guys a night can't deter your mood, even though I decided that the not caring thing would come easier if I drank with the little airplane bottles of liquor in my purse. Of course, I never had the nerve to do it in case I got caught. I had watched Melanie down some before a few shifts. She had a good reason though; she didn't have a license and since she had a designated driver to take her to work, which was me, it was somehow justified. It was a known fact that some people drank before their shifts, especially on slower nights just to pass the time I suppose or to relate to the drunks better that frequented the bar for hours every single day of the week. Eventually, one of the cocktail waitresses who I shared shifts with was promoted to a manager. I think it was because she wore glasses. Her glasses made her look responsible. She should have never been promoted. She had to kiss a lot of ass to get where she was; it was something I could have never done. I was almost jealous of people who could kiss ass so naturally. I was never a fan of kissing ass, which ultimately prevented me from keeping jobs past a certain point. It was worth it though; I didn't feel the need to respect somebody with a manager certification that didn't exist and a high school diploma which I myself had somehow managed to obtain. This particular manager usually only managed on Sunday nights because they were slow. She managed me and another girl bartender, Dawn. Football played all day on Sundays, and by the time the night game would arrive, people would be too drunk or falling into a nacho coma to watch it. These are the days they decided to put me on as a double. I loved working this shift because I got to wear a jersey and knee-high socks to match. It was a very, very 'original' uniform. I chose a Detroit Lions jersey. If you know anything about football, you know that the Detroit Lions can usually go a whole season without winning a single game. I'm pretty sure they have more records for losses than anything else and everybody who is not from Michigan chose to question my choice of jersey. This is exactly why I chose this jersey: it was a perfect conversation piece. Also, I thought I pulled off blue and silver pretty well. My other jersey was a Steelers jersey, and it was to accommodate the whole bar. People loved the Steelers or hated them but either way they were talking about them. Sundays were annoying and long. I would be forced to watch football all day long, every single game at once. If anybody needed to know every single score of every single football game at the same time, I would be the girl to ask. Nobody ever asked, which meant this knowledge was pointless. I had cocktailed before this job, but it wasn't full time, and it wasn't title worthy. This was a sports bar, so having sports knowledge was a plus. I was raised with two brothers and my dad who were all into sports. I started getting into them early on as a way to bond with them and I even started liking them. It was easy for me to talk to my tables about sports and anything else they wanted to hear. Some people would push too far by asking me to sit down with them. It wasn't degrading how they said it but the only other place I could think of that allows this behavior was Hooters. Hooters was one of the few places I had made my mind up early on to not work at quickly after getting into the industry. Mostly because I thought their famous wings were awful tasting. Oh, yeah, and even though I thought the orange and white would look great on my naturally darker skin, the cut would be more than unflattering on me. I know everybody says that the girls at hooters make bank, but there is no convincing me that construction workers, teenage boys, and UFC fighter fans are the ultimate tippers. I always made decent money without having to wear neon shorts and high-top tennis shoes. I remember there was this one time two guys started coming in on a regular basis. At the end of their meals, they would sometimes throw dollar bills up in the air. This was the closest I ever got to feel like a stripper. It was usually for their cocktail waitress, but once other cocktail waitresses caught wind, it became a money grab game. I, too, while having these guys in my section fell into the trance of watching them "make it rain". Sometimes, they would even rip the bills in half so that the cocktail waitresses would have to try harder. I stopped being a part of the money-grabbing game after this. The chances I was going to find both halves of the dollar bill with five other cocktail waitresses trying to find it, along with their dignity on the floor, seemed unlikely and felt like a lot of work for a dollar, or 50 cents if you weren't so lucky. The point being, they felt like they could pay you for their entertainment, and although most customers asked you to sit down rather than throwing dollar bills in the air, to me, it was almost the same concept. Paying me for my time. It was what my job was all about, but somehow this was now offensive.

While drowning ourselves in depression from moving to one hick town to another, Melanie and I decided maybe we needed a night to go out and forget about our problems that we really didn't have. Melanie and I met some girls at work that told us we should go to this bar downtown that consisted of a mechanical bull that gave you free rides and a bar top you could dance on. This description might've deterred some people but not us. In our hometown, when you go out, usually the girls wear heals and nice dresses. It was wintertime so Melanie and I put on our leggings and cute sweater dresses and headed out to meet our new coworkers at this place called Cowboy Playground. We also invited a friend to visit, our friend, Anne from back home, to share this new experience with us. Nothing could have prepared us for when we walked in the bar. We were overdressed. When I say overdressed, I mean we were wearing too many layers of clothing. To my left, there was a stage with a mechanical bull, to my right, there were barely 18 year old girls wearing see-through white wife beaters and blue jean shorts that I wished I could have fit in, back in the 7th grade. Above me, a clothing line that was used to hang laundry way back before I was born had bras hanging from it, lots of different colored, lacy bras. I wondered if this was decor or they had actually been worn by people, possibly people that were now dancing on the bar to copperhead road. Where were the night lights and the top 40 music playlist? My thought went to the bull. I was mad I had decided to wear a dress that night. Out of the three of us that went out that night, I was the only one legally old enough to drink, but this is when I didn't drink much, so I slipped my two friends a few sips of my house rum and coke so that we could all feel cool. Obviously, this did not give any of us a buzz, but for some reason, we thought we should go out and dance anyway. After the three of us split my one drink, we all three went out to the middle of the dance floor and started doing what I like to call the white girl dance. The white girl dance is when girls get together to dance but don't have any guys to dance with, so they form a circle and start doing stripper swirls up and down to the ground while occasionally pointing at their girlfriends. Kind of like "I see you dancing all pathetically alone over there, now watch me!!!" Then, you do the occasional run through your hair with your fingers to flip it in order to look sexy because somewhere along the line of growing up we were taught from music videos that guys like to see us flip our hair. I do think this is true, but only when our clothes are off. While doing this with clothes on, it looks like we have a serious lice problem that needs attending to every few minutes. So anyways, I was white girl dancing with my two friends, and it's very hard to white girl dance with only 3 people or odd numbers in general. We ended up forming a train where you grind up on your girlfriends to make guys think you're a lesbian and into all sorts of freaky stuff. When, we just don't know how to dance without grinding our asses on something. The last person in the train always gets screwed because she has to grind with air until a guy she doesn't want to approach her comes up and dances. He becomes the caboose to our train and the white girl dance is complete. Finally, guys start to take notice of our dance and come around. They look drunk, but I can't really tell because they are behind me. I make eye contact with Anne so that she can give me the thumbs up or down. She kind of makes a face. I am not sure if it's a good or bad face, so I keep dancing and then she starts pointing! Is she pointing at the guy or are we starting the white girl dance again but there are now guys involved, perhaps she doesn't get the rules. The other guy has Melanie on his shoulders until a security guard comes over and tells the guy to drop my friend. The song ends and the lights come on. Everybody starts walking out and then eventually we are all told to get out. Did we do something wrong? I look at my watch to see that it was 2 am, and although it felt that our night had just begun, it was all over at the same time. I looked to see where the guy dancing with me was. He was right behind me and he smiled. We all walked out of the club and I scream, "Hey where is the after-party at?" This is the first time I had been in a social setting since moving to North Carolina and wasn't even sure if this was socially acceptable behavior, but I didn't know anybody and wanted to hang out with new people and make friends. The guy screams out, "My house!"

Not knowing where My House was exactly, I asked him for his address. Perhaps a bit forward, I suppose, but my brother was our driver/security guard, and I thought if anything was going to go down, well, we would all go down together. Surprisingly, he gave us his address. I wondered if this was his first time giving out his address to a girl that he just met at a club. Anne thought this was a red flag. She seemed to think we should skip on the unofficial invitation to the after party I had just made up out of thin air.

"No way!" I said. "Plus, we asked him to come over! Do you think if he was a serial killer, he would wait for us to ask him his address to come over? That is a slick serial killer." Anne was not amused. After passing his house, we arrived almost an hour later. We knocked on what I had hoped was his front door. It took a while for anybody to answer, and I started to worry that he had given us "creeps" the wrong address. Finally, he answered the door and as we walked in. We saw a clean small tile area and stairs leading up to where he supposedly lived. Noticing that the stairs were clean, I asked him if we should take off our shoes and he replied, "Sure."

My brother, Melanie, Anne, and I all took turns taking off our shoes and started going up to the unknown in a line. I was third down. I still had a chance to run back down the stairs in case any foul play was to go down. As I got upstairs, I noticed a clean, almost sophisticated apartment. It had three bedrooms and was spacious and very clean. I must have commented that the place was clean five times, and said I was expecting more of a college boy dorm. He told me that he had already finished college in Michigan and worked here now and then told me his name was Joseph Hug. There was no way his last name was Hug; I asked to see his ID to see what kind of line he was using to possibly see my "I am a sure thing" panties I just had gotten from Victoria Secret.

His name was real and besides playing guitar hero completely sober, my brother passing out on his couch and Anne, Melanie, and I jumping in his bed with him, everything checked out as completely normal. Afterwards, Anne, Melanie, and I laid around him, trying to get to know the guy we had just jumped in bed with. It's not what you are thinking. This was one place we did not use the white girl dance or train, instead we all took turns asking him questions until 6 am quickly rose its obnoxious head. I was starving and wanted to introduce Anne to Bojangles on her first North Carolina visit. I watched the clock, hoping we could play 100 questions until it was time for them to open. I told him it was time for us to get breakfast, and he couldn't believe we hadn't already fallen asleep. I asked him if we would like to join us, but he said 24 hours of not sleeping was his limit, his loss. I started to walk out of his room, and he asked me for what else, a hug! Umm, sure, I can give you a hug. Up until that point, I didn't know if he was into me at all, but that made it clear, he obviously wasn't. We exchanged numbers, but I knew that I would probably never talk to or see him again.

CHAPTER ELEVEN
SUNDAY FUNDAY

After a weekend of getting crazy and eating way too much, it was Sunday again. As Sundays drew on so did my notice to my beyond giddy manager and fellow bartender I shared a shift with every Sunday. I loved the bartender and keep in touch with her to this day. Her name was Dawn. She was giddy, funny, quirky, outgoing, and funny. If she was ever in a bad mood, it was hard to tell. My manager, Olivia, started imitating the role of bartender on Sundays. She would help Dawn make drinks and entertain bar patrons. One time, I saw her pour shots while nobody was at the bar, quickly to be followed by them being tossed to the back of her throat. I knew this was grounds for being fired, but the thing that pissed me off more than anything was that I was the only one sober on the clock and she didn't even offer me a drink. The next few Sundays, Dawn and Olivia would take more chances and more shots. After a while, they began to ask me if I wanted one. I would always reply with a "no, thanks". I did want one. I wanted five. However, I was always afraid of getting caught, and I needed an income at this point in my life. One time I said forget it, what was the big deal? One shot in an almost empty bar wouldn't hurt anything. The bartender laid it on a table for me shortly after I sat down. I decided to pass on the shot and go greet the lady who just sat at my table first. Her name was Karma, and she was a bitch. As I was getting her drink order, she noticed Dawn and Olivia taking shots. She asked if that was okay. I didn't think it was a big deal, and this girl had an attitude problem. It was obvious that she was having a bad day, and I could see right through her motives. I tried to cover it up with "They shouldn't be doing that, but they probably just took one because a customer bought them a shot."

She then replied with, "It doesn't bother me, but you should just tell them it's probably not such a great idea. I'm not going to say anything." I went and told my tipsy manager who told me I was right and that they shouldn't be drinking. I'm pretty sure they finished up the evening with a few more shots. Not any sooner than the angry patron left, she contacted the owner of the place to let him know that his staff had been drinking on the clock the night prior. I know this because when I walked in the next day, I was asked to go straight to the office. I already knew what this was about, since I already had ten missed calls from my hung-over co-workers with ten scared voicemails. I got multiple calls begging me not to tell, that none of us would get in trouble if we all stuck together. The owner came in and specifically asked me why I didn't tell a manager. "I did, but the manager was the one drinking," is what I wanted to say. I didn't rat her out, and as for the no trouble thing, Dawn got fired. I got suspended for a week and threatened to be fired, and Olivia continued her life as normal. We looked less like a group than when Justin Timberlake decided to go solo. I was the only one who didn't drink that night and was now missing out on a few hundred dollars from those shifts. I decided that I hated my ignorant owner, and I would never lie for people again. If I have learned one thing from serving, it is that people are selfish.

However, my newfound hate for the owner wasn't new at all. I was one of, if not the best, cocktail waitress at this establishment. I worked harder than anybody on any given shift. I kept everything stocked and cleaned while other servers stood around talking and scraping empty ice bins. He once even had the nerve to call me lazy. He was clearly mistaken because, the lazier you were at this place, the better position you were offered. I remember there was this one girl I worked with; she was awful. She was lazy and did nothing to contribute to making the world a better place. She was the most incompetent server I had the displeasure of working with. She would watch everybody do her work around her without offering a helping hand. Every single person at this job was fed up with her behavior and habits. When it was time to do server evaluations on each other's performance, we were sure her days were numbered. Not a week later, after every server had called her out on her completely sucking, she was promoted to a floor manager. I wasn't surprised. She was everything a manager was supposed to be in a restaurant: somebody who had served before but now told everybody else what to do without having to do any work themselves. How classic, our plan had backfired, and like always, the world didn't make sense. Things only got worse at this job from there. I went on to be fired and rehired and fired again on my day off. Yes, the owner called me in on my day off, which happened to be New Year's Eve, to fire me. If I didn't have a reason to drink, then I certainly had one now. This was good because drinking without a reason can be reckless, but I also forgot that drinking without a job can be stupid. At the time, it all made sense, especially a few drinks in. Leading up to me being fired a second time, the owner had thrown a box of pan bread at Melanie because she forgot to give a couple at one of her tables their free pan bread we offered when anybody sat down. Another co-worker of mine had gotten into a heated argument with the owner over her supposedly giving her friends free drinks, which was entirely impossible. Being a server, you can't get drinks from the bar unless you have a ticket, which requires you to ring in the drink. This meant somebody would have to pay for them. His business was going under, and he was blaming everybody but himself. He even pinned that same girl against a pin ball machine at one point. I thought I might have to call the cops if he actually threw a punch. He was more than double her age. She threatened to sue him, and eventually, she too was fired on her day off. Sometimes, the owner would come into the bar and sit in the corner facing the wall and not talk to anybody. When I made my departure a second time, I pointed out the fact that he was a crazy asshole and his establishment deserved to be closed down. He just laughed at me. After I left, my roommate managed to stick around for another year. She would enlighten me with stories of how they had a meeting, and to prove a point, the owner threw his cellphone against a wall and as it laid dead on the ground, he asked a server to come up and step on it. When the server refused, he joked and said he needed a new phone. Needless to say, he no longer owns that business. You may ask why I had stayed as long as I did (on and off for two years. The money was good and I had made a lot of good friends. At the time, this was reason enough for me to stay. Not until my next job would I remember how a job is supposed to be and how managers were supposed to act, for the most part, anyway.

After Jackass Corporation, I didn't want to serve anymore. I know, you have heard this story before. I have ignored myself while listing out reasons why serving was no longer a good idea, but I also knew that after a few week break, and no tips, that I would be serving again.

JUST THE TIP

CHAPTER TWELVE
HI 5!

I can't believe I worked somewhere that was called HI 5. I can't believe I was shocked when this job didn't quite work out. After trying out a few different places surrounding my last place of employment, including right next door, I decided that my problem didn't lie in my lack of serving ambition but instead in the locations I was choosing to serve at. I wanted to venture out and try downtown. Perhaps a more urban area would offer a new outlook and energy that I was missing out on. While looking for a job, I did what anybody else now does: I made some food and clicked on Craigslist. The days of physically going out and meeting people to get a job is long gone, which I have to say I miss dearly. It has always been more my specialty to convince people in person that I am totally capable of doing whatever it is they want, and I am completely unable to prove it on paper. Every time I go on Craigslist, I always looked at the jobs that I can never get first and send them my resume just in case. That way, I don't feel like a complete loser when I'm clicking on the hospitality category for the 500th time. Anyway, I found this job on Craigslist. Perhaps this was another red flag? I was just glad it was in a building in a public area and not somebody's private kitchen. Either way, I was desperate enough to take the job. The ad read something like: High volume sports bar looking for cocktail waitresses. Yup! That's me. My resume was perfect for this. I deleted all the other fake secretary jobs I had put on there for the Administrative category on Craigslist and submitted my resume. I went in for an interview, and after waiting thirty minutes past the time I was supposed to be interviewed, the manager finally acknowledged my existence. This pissed me off. I almost walked out three different times before I was interviewed but was so glad I didn't. I got hired. They told me I would have to learn the 100 beers that they offered on their menu. They told me that their menu only consisted of five-dollar menu items (Hi 5? they should've called it low 5). The thought of a table of four only racking up a twenty-dollar check make me curl over in pain, and then to really knock me on my ass, the manager told me the uniform requirements. You must wear a black short sleeve button up shirt, a tie of your choice, a short plaid, pleated skirt, with matching knee-high socks. Oh, and if you can throw in pigtails and a lollipop, he would be sure to give you a boner, or did he say bonus? I can't remember. I do remember that I did not except the bonus offer but did take this opportunity to go shopping for some awesome knee-high socks. I even found some that glowed in black light that lined the club walls. You never know when you will need black light knee-high socks. I didn't realize how schoolgirl stripper I looked like until my daily walk to and from work. The constant question of "How much?" was yelled from passing car windows. Okay, I never heard them say that, but I am sure it was just hidden under the loudness of their car horns that they chose to beep at me continuously until I made it safely inside.

I didn't train long here because they didn't care. During the week, this place was completely dead. The "High Volume" in their ads should have been replaced with "High Hopes". It wasn't abnormal for me to walk away with twenty dollars in my pocket at the end of a night, and then there were the weekends. The weekends turned into a night club with a live D.J. that would broadcast live on air every Friday and Saturday night. These nights, we were extremely busy, but the money never showed it. The crowd was young, and the rest were just plain cheap. The fact that we offered a five-dollar menu until two a.m. at any place that involved alcohol was bound to cause issues, at least for the waitresses. I did get complimented on my socks quite a few times, mostly from college basketball players. They liked my swag, but they, too, didn't like to tip me. We had three levels of dance floors, and I felt like I was running around getting people drinks for free. Half the time, I wouldn't be able to ever find the people that ordered the drink in the first place. Besides a few black lights and light flashers, our club was completely dark. Rap music and broken glass pounded against our walls and floors just waiting until 2 a.m. where the underpaid cleaning crew (us) would come in to clean it up. The place was extremely small, but it always took us at least three hours to clean. I would walk out, with my schoolgirl outfit around 5 a.m. as the sun was coming up. I was making my walk of shame every night of the week, and since I was never up at 5 am to enjoy breakfast any other time, I decided to take advantage of my sucky night and spend money that I didn't make on McDonalds egg McMuffins. I hated my job. I hated how McDonald's breakfast started making me feel and look, and I hated that outfit. I went to bed around 7 a.m. after thinking about what tie and socks I would match together for a promising Saturday night.

I went in at 4 p.m. for my Saturday night shift, which would last until the typical 5 a.m. For my first few tables, I had the typical dinner crowd that all had small tabs, which meant small tips. It basically felt like I was waiting tables at a fast food restaurant, only with a horrible uniform. Around nine o'clock, we turned the lights down and prepared for our late-night transition. I was sat with five girls, probably all around twenty-one.

"Hi, how are you guys doing? Do you like my outfit?" I asked, knowing they would that be listening to what I said. They replied with, "Is everything on your menu really five dollars?"

"Yes, it is." The girls all ordered a Cosmo, or something that they saw on Sex and the City, and all ordered a five-dollar meal. I have to say, for five dollars, our meals were pretty good. I brought the girls their drinks. They weren't good.

"Why not?" I asked them.

"We don't want them," one of them told me.

"That's a horrible reason." After sending back their drinks and ordering new ones, their food arrived shortly after. They needed 5,000 ketchups, and 1,000 ranches and they couldn't decide this together as a whole, but each decided to order the same condiments only after I brought back the first round. This happened five times. About thirty minutes after dropping off their food, I asked them if everything was okay, and they ignored me. I took that as a yes, everything was okay. I didn't care about their forty-dollar tab and definitely didn't think I would have any complaints on decent food that went for five dollars a pop. I went to pick up their plates as I noticed one was only half-way touched.

"Um, excuse me! There was hair in my food."

I was completely over these bitches. I looked at her plate and small black curly hairs covered the entire top of her pasta dish. Neither my hair nor anybody else that I worked with had hair resembling what was scattered across her pasta dish like parmesan cheese. I told her I didn't think that hair was there when I brought it out and was so pissed that I openly blamed her. I thought she was going to get up and rip my own hair out. It would have made her case more probable, but she was stuck between three girls in a roundabout booth and just yelled at me instead. I picked up her pasta bowl, ran into the kitchen, and threw it on the line. When my manager came up and asked what was wrong, I said there was hair in her food. He took one look at the hair and made the same DNA assumption that I had. She ate half her food and just wasn't willing to pay five dollars for it. My manager didn't take it off, and I am pretty sure he told them to leave if they had a problem with his decision. They didn't leave, and I never approached the table again, even when they called my name, which they obviously thought was "Ma'am! Ma'am!"

I even saw some cash on the table when they were finally done sipping on their one drink each but left it for the bussers to fight over.

One night after leaving Hi 5, I decided to call Joseph. Surprisingly we had texted a few times since that first time we had met but had not seen each other since then. I called and let it ring a few times, nervous to hear his voice again. He finally answered in a lower, almost drugged-out like tone. Great, I thought. He was a stoner. I had nothing against people who smoked, but it wasn't one of the qualities I was looking for in a new boyfriend. I even asked him immediately if he was stoned. "It's three in the morning, why are you calling me?" I can't believe it never crossed my mind that perhaps this guy had a job with normal hours! I told him I just got off work and was feeling brave, so I decided to give him a call. I left out the feeling brave part on the phone. We only talked for a few minutes because he had to get up for work in three hours. I had never dated a guy who wasn't also in the industry with me up until that point. What was I saying? I hadn't even gone out on a second date, or any date for that matter, with this guy and now he was my new boyfriend who wasn't allowed to be stoned when I called at three a.m.? We made a date to meet up one night while his friend was in town visiting. I sat in the parking lot for 20 minutes deciding if I should go into the bar that we had agreed to meet in. I convinced myself that I shouldn't and decided driving away as fast as possible was my best option at that point until he said he would come out and meet me because it was taking so long. I told him I had gotten lost and that parking lots were very confusing. I got out, not quite sure if I would even remember what he had looked like. It had been a few months since I had seen him last. As he was walking towards me, I pinched myself a thousand times and almost kicked myself for not trying to meet up with him sooner. Joseph had almost a tan tint to his skin, brown eyes, black hair, and these long black eye lashes with just the right amount of beard shaved close to his face. He was around 6ft with a lean build. He was sexy, sexier than I had remembered. He gave me a smile; he had a great smile. I was glad he remembered what I looked like and then he said I looked great. I tried to hold in my excitement. I later confessed to him that I almost didn't get out of the car that night, and he said he was glad that I did. We went into the bar and sat in a booth with his friend, Chase, who was visiting from Michigan. At first the conversation was quiet, until I brought up White Castle. The one thing most northerners have an opinion about, good and bad. The conversation would have been much shorter if we didn't have things like hamburgers that came in mini suitcases to talk about. Joseph was wearing a chain around his left arm and a studded belt buckle. I'm such a sucker for detail. Usually I wouldn't be too hung up on chains or bling but for some reason this didn't bother me with Joseph but actually turned me on. He touched my leg; it turned me on. He smiled, it turned me on. Okay, you get the point. We left after a drink and headed back to his house where Chase enlightened me on stories of how he hooked up with Joseph's ex of five years and said that it would come up eventually. Really? When? It was not a question I had ever asked somebody. I didn't know if he was bragging or felt guilty with alcohol seducing him. Joseph seemed to be over it but quickly turned to me. "Are you over your ex?" he asked.

How did he know I had an ex, an ex that a few months prior I had an awful breakup with, who took my heart with him to

Florida? I, myself didn't know how I was standing there and in fact enjoying another guy's company. "Oh yeah... Completely, what are two years and a breakup via TEXT?" The truth was, I wasn't. He didn't need to know that and besides, without my permission, Joseph shortly changed that.

I only went to HI 5 a few more times after that. They eventually shut down. I think it was mostly because of their name.

I needed a change. What was I to do? Serving was all I ever knew up until this point. It was really by choice that I had turned my part time high school job into a six-year long career choice. This was okay during high school. It was okay during "college" which I had not attended, but now it was time for a big girl job. I was starting to feel older too. Sporting bright nail polish and earrings to make something out of my all black spandex uniform everyday was becoming very unflattering. I felt not mentally naive enough to serve anymore. I felt jaded and it was no one's fault, but at the same time everyone's.

CHAPTER THIRTEEN
PIZZA AND SEX ARE GOOD, BUT NOT AT THE SAME TIME

When Joseph, my newfound love interest, suggested I get a serving job at this pizza bar that he and his friends frequented on a weekly occasion, I was a little skeptical. For some reason, a pizza joint seemed less glamorous than the already not so glamorous part-time job I had made into a full-time career. That and when Joseph thought to bring this up to me, it was over the phone, with one of the owners in the background asking if I had nice boobs. If this was the interview, I knew I had it hands down, but what had my life come to?

"How is your pizza, beer, and my boobs? Are they all to your liking? Great." I needed a job and I wanted Joseph, and if this meant I would get to see both, I decided I had to take it.

Before starting, I asked Joseph if there was anything, I should know about this place that the owner so eagerly recommended me for after meeting me and my boobs. He said it was a cool joint that usually got busy on the weekends. He then told me that the bartender was a bitch. I didn't know why I needed to know this but was thankful for the heads up. I instantly asked if she was pretty, I was suddenly insecure. He said she was okay, nothing great, and that I won that battle hands down. Who said I was trying to battle? "Basically, she will be a bitch to you because you are a girl," he said.

Great. What did I do to this girl? She was mad that some people, other than her, were blessed with a vagina? It was such a lame excuse not to like somebody, but as soon as I met her, I knew why she was like that. Sarah was the only girl bartender that I knew of working at this establishment that would be working with me. She wasn't very good at her job, but they probably kept her back there because she was girl-next-door cute, and it went well with the neighborhood appeal this place had. Sarah was very petite, (her only appeal in my opinion) around 5'3" with short brown hair. If anybody can picture "mousy" I would kind of describe her like that. She had nice teeth, but she never smiled, and her face passed for okay. I could tell mentally she was unsteady when, on my first week there, there were multiple nights I found her crying in the boss's office or out by the dumpster when I took out the trash. I never said anything, but in my mind, I wrote her off as being crazy and insecure, or insecure because she was crazy. I wasn't sure which one and I didn't care.

The first few weeks there were good. This place was not as big as the other restaurants I had worked at, but the bar and patio were very appealing to watch any game. This bar was always crawling with regulars who lived around the area, mostly guys. It reminded me of a pizza place that I used to eat at every time we won a basketball game in the 4th grade. I never really contributed to the win, except for one time when I stole the basketball and made a basket, only to find out I had shot it in our basket. The money wasn't amazing, by any means, but the place was so casual it was nice to just wear shorts and a T-shirt and not have to look like a raving sex kitten to deliver beers and beg for tips. I also got out at nine or ten o clock every night which was a far cry from the three a.m. I was used to for the last four years. I fought between not making any money and getting out early, and somehow in my pea of a brain, the getting out early side won. I would soon realize getting out early made it impossible to pay my bills early or even late for that matter. Joseph and his friends would come in and order pizza and beer on the weekends before a night out on the town. Sometimes they would sit with me, and others they would sit at the bar. I never understood why passing me to fight for a seat at the bar where a mediocre, bitchy, vagina hater was waiting to frown at you for ordering a beer was ever an option. At this point, Joseph and I were seeing each other more frequently, but when he would come in, I felt like a crazy girlfriend who had to try to get his attention. I didn't think anything about it other than I am a girl and we are crazy. This was all I knew after leaving high school to be true. It was Joseph who would act way too casual for my liking. He would say bye when he left in a tone that made me think we should throw a high five to each other or do chest bump. I never liked chest bumps, they hurt. I'm sure Joseph would like it. One time I even followed him out to his car to ask for a kiss. He reluctantly gave me one. I was mad that I had to work every single weekend night and that a date between us consisted of me going to sit on his couch to watch Family Guy until he fell asleep at ten p.m. in order to get up for his "real job" every morning. I decided to take my mind off of boys and focus more on work. Soon after meeting everybody that I would soon spend five days a week with, I met Ana. Ana was awesome. I soon realized that she also bartended and served here. Her personality beat Sarah's hands down, and I wondered why she didn't get the better bar shifts. Ana was about my height with a thicker build. She had short, wavy black hair and pale skin. She seemed like she was raised in a very structured environment, but she had a carefree soul. Ana was funny and gave off an attitude of not giving a shit. I'm instantly drawn to these types of people. She didn't like Sarah. In fact, nobody really did, but nobody ever said anything. Ana told me how she used to be engaged, but at the last bar she worked in, she met and fell madly in love with one of the cooks. She said she had graduated college and that her fiancé had done the same. They had their lives planned out to be what looked like perfect, even her family had hoped marriage was in their future. She said somewhere deep down she knew she wasn't being fully fulfilled with her relationship. The summer before they were supposed to get married, she went on a road trip with her girlfriends to Montana. She said it was life changing. I personally couldn't imagine Montana being life changing, but it made me want to drive out there to find out for myself. If Montana was selling life changing plans, it was something I was definitely interested in investing in. I liked how open Ana was, too open sometimes. Ana told me about how Sarah and one of the owners were having a fling, which everybody knew but were supposed to pretend they didn't. Sarah sucking all of a sudden made sense. In walks Chris. Chris was always in the bar, sometimes working, most of the time just drinking. Chris was always nice to me. Chris was the son of one of the owners, which in turn made him the owner of this particular location. Chris was about 5'11", decent build, black, spiky hair that was always kept pretty long, brown eyes, and olive toned skin. He was probably in his later 30s, but his face looked a little worn, even for his age. I blamed the drinking and other habits he was into, rumors that had been circling around me since starting here. After Ana told me about Sarah and Chris, it was so obvious why she had the best bar shifts, why she was allowed to suck at her job, and why she hated "her man" hiring any other attractive females. She was at least ten years younger, still in college, and working part time. He was older but not more mature. He liked to drink in his spare time and lived in a house with his two kids and wife! How had I not noticed before? His wife would come in and sit at the bar while Sarah tried to win her over with good service and funny stories. She tried to be her friend to hide the fact that she was in fact her husband's girlfriend. I told Joseph about it, and he said that he knew something was going on, or at least always assumed. I thought it was very entertaining.

One day when I was working, Joseph and his friends came in on a Friday night. They sat outside because the weather was nice, and I was their server. Shortly after getting their drink orders, Sarah walked in and walked past me and smiled. That was weird, she never smiles. Maybe she's trying. I returned with their pitcher of beer to see Sarah sitting next to Joseph. Was this some kind of fucking joke? I looked at him, like what the fuck are you doing? He looked at me like, I'm doing exactly what you think I'm doing, only I'm going to make it look as casual as possible so you look crazy if you overreact. Perhaps I was overreacting, they came in all the time. Perhaps she was hanging out with some people that came to the bar who she was familiar with to keep herself occupied while her boyfriend was having a family dinner with his wife. Okay.

"What can I get you guys to eat?" Joseph got the cheese sticks, and Sarah didn't want anything but a drink. Everybody else got a grinder sandwich or calzone. I didn't care what everybody else got. I cared what Joseph was trying to get. I brought his cheese sticks, only to find when I went outside to refill their waters, he and Sarah were sharing them. I was furious. How dare he openly flirt with a girl I found pathetic and unstable, but not only that, in my section while I waited on them! I rarely went back to the table after that and ignored him when they left when he tried to give me a kiss. No, I will not kiss you as you are about to go out with another girl and four drunk witnesses that you call your friends. Now I had a reason to not like Sarah, but my reasons would soon double within the next few shifts.

Chris came in to have a few drinks with friends one night only to have Sarah join him outside for some company after she got off her shift. She always managed to get off when he was around. I wanted to get off, too, but not with him around. I was having a really bad shift. There was a softball tournament in town and what seemed like hundreds of kids were taking up the entire patio. Nobody wanted to stay in their seats, making it impossible for me to match any kid to any parent, which made it impossible to figure out checks. I just knew I would have to pay for whatever was left over, and at this point, the checks that had not been claimed added up to more than I would make in two nights. I wanted to cry. I was also waiting on Chris and Sarah. I told Chris I was about to cry, and he told me to sit down for a minute. SIT DOWN?! The patio was falling apart, and he wanted me to relax. I sat down, hoping he was cool enough to order me a few shots. He wasn't. Somehow, he thought my behavior was like Sarah's. It must have been the "I want to cry" comment. Other than that, we had nothing in common. Chris laughed and said, "Well, you might not have a lot in common, but you both like to sleep with the same guys." What was he talking about? I wasn't sleeping with him. Was this an invitation? Ew. I just stood up and walked away. For a boss, he didn't make my night better; it was almost like he tried to make it worse on purpose. What kind of owner was this? Oh, yeah, one that slept with college girls while his wife took care of their kids. Around the same time, Joseph and his friends came in and sat down inside. They were also at one of my tables. I told them about my night and how shitty it was and what Chris had said to piss me off. They all looked at me in silence and then it hit me. I flipped out.

"Joseph! Did you and Sarah sleep together? YOU ARE DISGUSTING!"

"Can we talk about this later?"

"LATER?!?? No, we cannot." He kept ignoring me until he finally decided he should leave instead of manning up. I was devastated. I somehow finished my shift and went home, deciding I would never go back again. Not to serve pizza or beer, and especially not to serve as somebody's idea of entertainment. I needed the money. I went back, but I worked less and less. I ended up talking to Joseph about it, and he said it had happened way before he knew me and that he didn't think it was his place to tell me about something that happened when I didn't exist in his life. Everybody else confirmed this story as well. The way Chris had made it sound was like it happened recently. I know he did it on purpose, but I didn't know why. I eventually forgave Joseph, but I still didn't like the fact he thought I should work with a girl he had slept with, as if it would never come up.

One night after work, Ana, Chris, Sarah, and some other coworkers were having drinks after work during karaoke night. They asked me if I wanted to join. If Ana wasn't there, I would have given them the finger and walked away, but I decided I needed a drink more than my pride at this point. A lot of drinks. A few hours later at close, some of the coworkers stayed after hours to get some free drinks on the house. I was about to leave when Sarah told me I should follow her home, so we weren't driving separately drunk. I thought this was the stupidest idea I ever heard of. "Okay! Sounds great!" Shit, drunk Tonya always thinks every idea is great. I was mad drunk Tonya decided to join me on a night like this. Everybody left. Chris said he was staying for a while to work on paperwork, and I got in my car and followed Sarah into a fucking circle! She circled the parking lot and parked exactly where we had just left. Was this some kind of joke? I got out of my car to try to understand where Sarah's head was at. Or where mine was. Was I that drunk? She said it was just a trick to get everybody to leave so we could continue drinking with Chris. I thought this was a horrible idea, but drunk Tonya was all about it. I went in to have another drink when Chris and Sarah informed me that sometimes they spent the night in a booth and turn on the jumbo screen to watch television. I felt like I was in weird movie. Perhaps it was time for me to leave.

"You can sleep in this booth, Tonya! It's the most comfortable."
What an honor I thought to myself.

"Oh, that's okay, I have a bed at my house in which I'm allowed to sleep in with other people. You and Sarah have a good night!" I shouldn't have driven home, but I had to go somewhere. I didn't know if that night was leading to somebody's fantasy playing out in front of me, or if they were actually really worried about me receiving a DUI. I imagined it was the first. Sarah and Chris didn't seem like they worried about much but each other. The next day, I asked Chris how he slept. He said Sarah had left shortly after me (sure, she did) and that he brushed his teeth in the back sink this morning and felt like shit. I imagined feeling the same if I had slept in a booth with a girl I was having an affair with. I didn't stay at this job for more than a few months. I was getting my hands onto more drama than tips and that wasn't my point of working. Chris just wasn't a good boss, mostly because his personal life overtook his ability to do his job, that and the drug habit I mentioned earlier that was only a rumor. It wasn't that Chris wasn't nice, he was. I even heard that he eventually bought Sarah the boobs she had been wanting. Right then, I realized it wasn't my vagina she was mad at; it was my boobs I liked to carry around with me all the time. I later saw them when they came out to dinner to a new place I was employed at downtown. I immediately looked at her boobs and decided that neither she nor her boobs were worth the money. Chris and his wife eventually divorced. I can't imagine why.

JUST THE TIP

CHAPTER FOURTEEN
WHAT IS A GASTROPUB?

One day, Melanie and I were walking the streets of downtown, looking for our big girl jobs that we were both unqualified for. I had the confidence to pull it off, but the experience would be harder to fake. Perhaps, I had watched Erin Brockovich too many times. I loved that movie for two reasons. One, it was based on a true story and two, if she could fake being a lawyer based on having a smartass attitude and nice rack, I knew this job thing would be easier than I had first thought. After all, my rack was just as good if not better than hers.

"Would you like one, Tonya?" Melanie asked, interrupting my daydream, as we stood by a hot dog stand near the courthouse. As much as I build myself up, I wasn't sure if I could Erin Brockovich my way into a partner position at a law firm, not yet at least. Hopefully, Hell will eventually freeze over. Directly across the street was a Gastropub. Right beside the Gastropub was a group of homeless guys whose attention was stuck on the TV that was permanently placed outside the news station. This may have deterred some people from checking this side of the street out, but I was curious to find out exactly what a Gastropub was.

As we walked by, the homeless people started speaking to us, only it didn't sound like English. It was some gibberish that somehow they understood between themselves and we didn't. They all started laughing. I was sure they had no idea what was going on, plus I had plenty of experience with homeless people. In Richmond, you knew them by name, or by corner. I usually helped out when I could, but one day I was approached at least ten times, I was so fed up with being asked for money that when a young guy approached me with some story about his band's van being broke down, without letting him finish, I threw change in his cup. "Hey! That was my coffee, you jerk!"

Oh, my God. He wasn't homeless, he was just asking for some help. I walked away completely embarrassed as he wiped coffee splatter from his hands. That was the thing about Richmond, VA; you never knew who was actually homeless because everybody wanted to look homeless there. It was considered stylish not to shower or wash your hair. I could tell this place was going to be different and that if you looked homeless, you were more than likely homeless. I'm talking about homeless as in sitting on a bench screaming obscenities, having more conversations with yourself than anybody else, and asking for money because you claim that you are hungry but yet food offerings are looked down upon. Melanie and I quickly walked past the homeless guys with only a few hoots and hollers trailing after us. I never felt more attractive than when being hit on by a homeless guy. My mom would be so proud. I have been asked out by numerous homeless people before; I wondered where they would take me if I had ever agreed to go on a date with them. Would I be stuck paying? What would we eat? How many unknown benches around the area would I be introduced to that I had no idea had existed? Somehow this rang true for other dates I had been on and decided that the guys I chose to date were almost on the same level as a homeless guy but smelled better. I made a note to myself to get better standards. We finally made it to the Gastropub and walked in to check it out. As we walked in, there was a beautiful fish tank that took up the entire back wall of the hostess stand but there was no hostess. To the right, there was a room with a ceiling that seemed to change colors with every move you made. To the left was a warmly lit bar in colors of red and oak wood. You would think Melanie and I had not been out in public before, especially in such a fine establishment. I admit, we hadn't in a while, due to the fact that we were jobless and had no driving privileges between the both of us until recently, having regained access to a vehicle and getting our self-respect back. Without having anyone to help us, we took it upon ourselves to explore on our own. We checked out the dining room, which was empty. We sat on the leather couches in the parlor as if we hadn't seen a couch before and then made our way to the bathrooms. You can tell a lot about a person by their bathroom. I was treating my job search more like a background check for a love interest rather than a place of employment. Everything seemed to check out. I had to pee. That checked out too. As I made my way to the bar in hopes of catching some form of life while being there, Melanie had already made herself comfortable with a Cosmo in hand. Ah HA! Somebody had serviced Melanie....I hope. "Isn't this place cool? We should hang out here sometime!" As oppose to what we were doing now.

I reminded her that I would like to hang out here a lot, approximately forty hours a week, and I would like them to pay me for hanging out. I asked for a job application and Melanie's check all at once. I didn't think getting drunk prior to filling out an application would be smart or very Erin Brockovich of me. As we walked out, it had hit me. I just filled out an application to serve, again. It was inevitable that this would remain my fate until perhaps I won a lottery that I never played or ended up on a reality show that was not based on any reality I knew of.

The next few days would be different, though. With my experience, I just assumed I would get the job or didn't care either way. This time I got no call back. I waited a few days. Nothing. With other jobs, I would have just blown it off and looked elsewhere, but the idea of going back to a sports bar after experiencing plush leather couches and star covered ceilings was just not an option. The fact that this job didn't have interest in me only made me want it more. Was I not good enough for this job? I must have called them at least four times to set up my own interview. After the fourth time asking when I could come in to speak to somebody without being invited, the managers were all out of excuses and agreed to see me. I got hired on the spot. I went in the next day to fill out mandatory paperwork and showed proof of I.D. My first day I was greeted with a hyper-active manager who seemed to be bothered by my presence. He was only general manager for my first three days there, but I later found out he liked to spend most of his shifts in the bathroom due to a white powdery substance he had become very fond of. The next two general managers also failed due to their love of not wanting to be at work. I stopped worrying about our weekly general manger change and met my veteran server I would be training with.

I met Jack. He was a young, blond guy around thirty. Although I had been through the training process a million times before, this time it felt different. Jack seemed to thoroughly enjoy his job, which in a restaurant in the middle of the week is hard to find. Even when his tables were beyond disrespectful, he kept his cool with them and me. He was good at his job and made good money. His fresh outlook on making it fun to serve people made me remember why I got into serving in the first place. I had gotten into this industry based on the fact that somebody once told me I could make money by bringing people food and engaging in twenty different conversations a night. I once loved meeting new people and now didn't even want to make eye contact with another human being while entering Target. It's like I thought if somebody noticed me noticing them, they would ask me for something. I wanted to make waitressing fun again and decided to have a change of heart. Jack was personable, witty, and very humorous. He would have me laughing along with his tables all night. That's the other thing I remembered about serving, I love making people laugh. I personally believed if you could make your table laugh at least once during their stay, it automatically increases your tip. I have even tipped servers who weren't very good based on the fact that they made me laugh and made my time more enjoyable. Tables usually love that, it's like free entertainment that you have to pay for. My high on becoming the server I had always hoped to be was crushed minutes after my first table was seated. None of them made eye contact with me. In serving, it becomes extremely alarming on how much you start to read your tables based on how they look or within moments of meeting them. It's even scarier to find out that, ninety percent of the time, you are right. I walked up to my table of four women, all probably in their mid-forties. I asked them what they would like to drink. Immediately, I get a special request for bottled water, since one of the ladies will not drink tap water. Understandable, I think to myself, while also thinking that this table may be a top running candidate for my most high maintenance table. As I was walking away from the table with less needy drink orders from the other ladies, the bottled water lady let me know that she also needs a cup of ice on the side. I wonder if she knew our ice was formed from tap water. Surely, she knew Pellegrino didn't make ice cubes. I returned to the table with their tap water and more prestigious water in hand. They informed me they were ready to order food; this being the next step in the food service process I agreed. Pellegrino told me she would like a cheeseburger with no cheese. I scratched the cheeseburger out and just left burger on my notepad. She also wanted no bun, light on the mayo on the sandwich but extra mayo on the side, add bacon that was well done, but insisted that her burger be rare, preferably bleeding, and as her side she wanted fries minus the potatoes. (Okay, the last part wasn't true) but she finished with an "I don't mean to be difficult." She was difficult and I was hoping her tap water friends wouldn't follow in her footsteps. One of the other ladies ordered a simple salad, with added salmon, but her last friend ordered the roasted chicken, which included smashed potatoes, broccoli, red peppers, and, of course, chicken, which the whole name was based on. She modified it to the point that the chicken didn't even exist in the dish. It somehow transformed into our fish and chips, no chips, add a baked potato and asparagus. I started scribbling out everything I had written down to begin with and just wrote, "bitch" instead. Melanie once made a comment about how she wondered if serving would ever get so bad that she would have a personal request to feed people by hand. This situation also made me think of this and I was weary that these ladies might be the first to try and get away with it. I wondered why difficult people were always apologizing for being difficult. Were they really sorry? Their tips never made me believe otherwise. Somehow, the food came out mediocre. Maybe their marriages had been mediocre, maybe their entire lives were mediocre, and I was to blame for everything that I had nothing to do. This fresh new outlook was going to be difficult with the same old attitudes. I decided to not let it deter me quite yet.

As a kid, were you ever asked, if you could have any superhero power, what would it be? I always remember wanting to have two superhero powers: one was to be invisible and the other was to be able to fly. I'm happy to say that I have accomplished both in my life, and I can say that both powers suck. I rather drive than fly, and when I'm talking to somebody, I would like them to acknowledge that I am there. As soon as I started training, I knew this place was going to be different than what I was used to. I was turned off by the stuck-up crowd that chose to socialize here. Co-workers would comment on how I shouldn't care if the people were stuck up. They were people that were here to spend money and we were here to make money. The attitude of emotionally shutting off completely is always something I had trouble with, and when somebody was disrespectful, I took it personally.

A few shifts in, I approached a table of five business guys. I assumed they were business guys because they were all wearing suits and kissing up to the one guy at the end of the table who must've been their boss. Within two minutes after being seated, all five guys were deep in conversation. I wish people would just wait until after the waitress does her job. Anybody who has been out to eat knows that in a matter of time, your server will be standing at your table, expecting drink orders. I approached them, anyway.

"Hi, how are you guys doing?" I asked.

Nothing. Sixty seconds later...Nothing. Not one person even looked up at me. This is where I usually talk really loud over the cocky boss and ask for drink orders, and they usually all look at me like I'm the one who is being rude, as if this wasn't my place of employment, but sometimes, sometimes I like to just stand there and see how long it will take them to notice a human being standing at their table, how long for them to acknowledge me and let me do my job. This happens a few times a night, especially on a busy night. If they make me stand there for longer than an hour, I walk away without saying anything. Okay, not really. One-minute tops and I'm walking. Do you know how awkward it is to stand at a table with nobody looking at you with others around wondering why I'm standing there? As I snap out of my thoughts that I'm writing you now, I realize they are still talking, and it's not directed at me. I decide to leave. Not even one minute after I leave, do I see a guy from the table get up and flag me down.

"Hi, do you know who our waitress is? We need to order." Of course, you do. Let me introduce myself, my name is Tonya. I was just here for five minutes, and you didn't notice, also you won't remember my name and will ask another waitress for your check forgetting I have brown hair and not blonde. What can I get you? I knew I would be seeing a lot more of "these people" here. After all, I was in a Gastropub, meaning, a pub that served higher quality food. We were also in the heart of downtown, across the street from the courthouse and two blocks from the convention center. Most of the people I would be waiting on would be from out of town, I presumed. My first two weeks there, I had never seen that many suits in one place except at a wedding or funeral, where it was practically required. My favorite parts of these men were their lack of social skills and personality. They were never funny and almost always socially awkward. I always said I'd rather be a server with a personality than a corporate robot. They always seemed to be on a schedule, and I sometimes wondered if they even had to schedule times to have sex with their wives, assuming they had wives. I always found it really inhumane to be rude to somebody you just met, which they seemed to have no trouble with.

A few tables later, I am seated with three intoxicated women, but it's okay because they are drunk off of our half- priced bottle wine night, and wine is sophisticated. These ladies were anything but sophisticated. I approached them, afraid to ask them what they would like to drink, afraid they would take advantage of the special and order another bottle of wine. Before I even introduced myself, I was interrupted with, "Shiraz, and we need food."

Of course, because everybody knows that food soaks up alcohol (not completely true). I go to put in their order when I hear a loud screeching noise from across the bar. It almost sounds like a human's voice, a lady's voice. Oh shit, it's my intoxicated table. "Hey! Hey!"

I look at her in shock; this is a grown ass woman screaming across the entire restaurant in an octave range. This must be very important. I run to her rescue in case she happens to be dying.

I get there and she lets me know that they will also need three waters, which obviously couldn't have waited. Perhaps, she needed the water and wine to wash down some medication, maybe it was mediation that was not supposed to be mixed with alcohol. I brought them their wine and water and scanned the table for pills; there were no pills in sight. The food ended up not being good enough for them. After asking what I recommended, they went with the only things that I didn't mention. After all, I had no idea what I was talking about, I only work there. The good thing about this place, besides everybody being better than me was that most of the time, was that the clientele here tipped twenty percent.

Many of my friends and acquaintances are shocked to find out that people in the service industry don't receive paychecks. Just to put it out there because some people may not know, servers make $2.43 an hour in most places, unless you live somewhere with a higher cost of living. Yes, the mark after the two is in the correct place. It is not abnormal for all my checks in a year to have, 'This is not a check', stamped across it. TIPS used to mean To Insure Proper Service. People would tip beforehand to insure good service was guaranteed to them. I wish I could give service based on a preview of what my tip was going to be first. I'm sure my tips would increase greatly only after a few bad previews.

This reminded me that at my first serving job one particular table of five people would always come in and always suck. Every server hated seeing them walk through the door, and when I finally got the pleasure to serve them, they didn't disappoint. I gave them good service, thinking like I always do, that I was going to change the world, one appetizer, one dinner, or one dessert at a time. They left me a single penny on their departure facing up. My friend who was bartending at the time informed me that leaving a penny faced up was an old tradition of basically saying you suck. This table wasn't too old. What? Did they research this tradition first? I became so enraged that I took the penny and the other change they left for the rest of their bill, walked out into the parking lot and tapped on their window. They gave me the finger, and I threw my handful of change against their glass as hard as I could as they drove off. I wish I could say that was the only altercation I had in a parking lot. A few years later, at a corporate chain restaurant, I was told by a manager to run after a walk out, I on foot, them on wheels, unless I wanted to pay for their bill myself. Since the idea of paying for a complete strangers' meals seemed very unappealing, I ran after them on the road to a stoplight in which I tried to write down their license plate number and failed miserably. You would think my boss would have appreciated my efforts and the loss of recent calories and rewarded me of some sort; she rewarded me with a fifty-dollar bill that was unpaid. I bring this back up, because as much as I would like to say this behavior was something of the past, something in my immature years of serving, I would be lying. I would relive this exact feeling of insanity a few months into my most recent serving job.

It was a normal dinner shift in the dining room with people who were pickier than usual. I managed to keep my cool all night until a guy called me over to his table, which I was not serving. I asked him what I could help him with. He started rubbing his hands lightly up and down my arm. Confused and about to punch him in his face, I noticed an unidentified long hair lying across my arm. Grossed out by the fact that the hair was not mine and that the guy felt the need to use my arm for a showcase made me outraged. He then let me know that he found the hair in his appetizer of wellington bites. I informed a manager that the psycho handing out free DNA strands would like to speak to him. This whole situation made me late to introduce myself to my next table. I approached my table of five younger adults, three girls and two guys all probably still in college. They all ordered drinks and appetizers to start. One of the guys ordered the wellington bites. After explaining to him that they were not your typical wellington bites, even with hair strands removed, he decided to still give them a try. As soon as I brought the appetizers, the girl who must have been sleeping with the guy who ordered the wellington bites suddenly had a look of disgust on her face and soon became the asshole I knew she could be. She then asked me what he had ordered, feeling like a broken record, I repeated myself, saying the exact same thing before the order had been placed. She insisted what we were selling were not beef wellingtons (they weren't, they were wellington bites) and made me take them off the table. Her boyfriend said it was fine and made me put them back on the table. She told me they didn't want them, that she knew what beef wellingtons were, and that these were not them. She was right. These were not your typical beef wellingtons, and if her head had not been so far shoved up her own ass twenty minutes prior, she would have known this. I suddenly frustrated with her talking to me like an idiot said, "I don't know why you are yelling at me. I didn't make this menu or this food!"

How dare I speak to her in the same tone she was using with me, her friend looked at me in anger.

"Excuse me! How dare you talk to us like that? We need to see your manager!" In total shock that this conversation ever had to take place any time in my life and after being treated like a scolded child from girls who were obviously physically and mentally younger than me, I yelled, "I'll get my manager. You guys are unreal! Do you think I care if I lose my job? I'm a server! I can find a million other serving jobs. I'll be right back."

I walked away with a second of gratification only to be followed by a nervous, anxious feeling. The truth was, I did care. I liked my job and went up to my boss to tell him that I was pretty sure I just fired myself and that he needed to go see my table. The worst part being that my general manager was now Jack, who had worked his way up from a server position with me in the beginning. When he asked me what the problem was, for the second time I said, "It's those damn wellington bites again!"

After talking with the table, Jack agreed that they were rude and stuck up but informed me if I ever acted out like that again at a table, I would have to be terminated. I was glad I wasn't fired for two reasons. 1. I liked my job and 2. I had won a free trip to Vegas at our annual Christmas party a few months prior and was pretty sure it was only redeemable if you were still employed.

JUST THE TIP

CHAPTER FIFTEEN
QUARTER PAST 1 A.M.
AND NO DRINKS IN...

After an exhausting weekend in Vegas, where I managed to get kicked out of the newest hotel and night club on the strip by jumping into a pool, fully clothed, with five girls from Australia who also thought pools were for swimming in, a total of six hours sleep in three days and one fake twenty-first birthday later, it was time to return to reality: working. I started to cocktail at the Gastropub; it was more suited to my kind of personality. I find it sad that I relate better to people that are more than a few drinks in, rather than somebody who is completely sober. Also, the bar was high volume, and you got a nine-table section to yourself during the week, which meant more money. Dinner still ran on both sides during the weekdays and weekends, but at ten p.m. on the weekends, the servers were cut and sent home with most of their sanity intact while cocktail waitresses on the other hand, were left to fend for themselves. After ten is when all the social butterflies would come out, mostly meaning alcoholics, and in this particular establishment, frat guys and sorority girls that got wasted every weekend and always ended their stay with a trip to the bathroom stall, where they would run out of vomit way before they had actually reached the toilet seat. I had to give them credit for trying and the fact that they always managed to leave a disgusting trail of dinner leftovers, making it easy for their equally wasted friends to find them, was something to admire. We had live music on Fridays and Saturdays; these were our busiest nights and the nights that we stayed open until 2 a.m. These were the shifts that you wanted to work. You had the opportunity to make a lot of money, and if you managed to keep your sanity being the only sober person in a room of about 200 wasted people, it promised to be rewarding. I never understood why I was determined to be at a bar until 2 a.m. without a drink in hand. Every shift I felt like I was watching a video from our adolescence classes, saying this is your brain on booze and if it wasn't for the no cell phone rule on the clock at work, I'm sure I would hold the record for the most viewed YouTube videos in history. The atmosphere was fun. I was getting paid to listen to live music, get people wasted, and make fun of them all at the same time. Sound too good to be true? I know. I thought so, too, but these jobs do exist. Once again, my parents must be proud. I finished my Friday night shift my first week back from Vegas with some cash in my pocket, my feet aching from standing up for 10 hours straight, and unable to escape the smell of vomit in my nasal cavity. I immediately jumped in the shower when I get home and mentally prepared myself for another night. There are only 13 more hours until my next shift. This isn't enough time.

As I go into my Saturday night shift, I notice it is dead. I'm the 4 o'clock shift, which usually means I get all the tables until the other girls come in. In this case, it looked like I would be standing around wishing I had been scheduled at a later time and thinking about how far away 3 a.m. seemed. About an hour after my arrival, with one more table under my belt than them, the 5 o'clock and 6 o'clock arrive. We took turns taking the scattered dinner tables that came in, but it never got busy enough to keep us busy. I took my phone into the bathroom and started texting friends hoping they would visit, hoping they would bring money. It was highly unlikely that any of them would respond. I would try to bribe them by saying we had a live band, but we always had a live band, and my friends' taste in music was hardly the cover band that was playing. Now, if I could get half of their sets to be rap and the other half to be country, maybe...no, they still wouldn't show. Soon, even though I never thought it was going to happen, it was ten o'clock. Ten o'clock started our late night; it was what I most and least looked forward to all at once. Ten o'clock meant everything was about to go to hell, but it also meant that I only had five more hours of work left. My late-night section started filling up in the dining room with mostly water drinkers and late-night food orders. I hated that 1 a.m. seemed reasonable for people to order their dinner, but, then again, I myself had fallen victim to this meal plan before, only after hanging out with my friend Captain Morgan and his life partner, Coca-Cola. We had some good times together, but we have been on the outs lately. I don't want to talk about it. After losing all morale and knowing it was completely impossible to hope that none new would walk through the door for the rest of the night, I had one table sit that didn't promise to be anything special, but anything was better than the nothing I had endured all night long. It was three older people, a guy and two women, all probably in their fifties. Although they didn't act like it, I could tell the guy was completely wasted. He almost fell asleep three times while ordering and waiting for his food to arrive, but somehow managed to finish his food and drinks and asked for his bill. It was the highest bill I had all night, around one hundred and twenty dollars. He gave me cash and handed me one hundred and forty dollars, not knowing if the extra twenty dollars was my tip, which I was hoping was. I gave him back his change, hoping in his drunken state he would still leave a good tip. I watched him stare at his check for what seemed like thirty minutes and then he eventually left. I ran over to the book expecting to find something way less than I was praying for, and to my surprise, he had left me the twenty but not only that twenty, about seven twenties. This couldn't be right. I started questioning myself and wondering if he had even paid the bill in the first place. I remember giving him back his change, I looked over his check again, and he had paid me the same amount he had the first time that I picked up the book. I ran to the kitchen to tell my co-workers that I'm pretty sure I had just witnessed my first small miracle and prayed he wouldn't realize his mistake and come back. He was so drunk that he had paid the same bill twice. He left me a one-hundred-and-sixty-dollar tip on a one-hundred-and-sixty dollar bill. This never happens or has happened to me again. It's a shame. I think more people should come in that are drunk from drinking doubles all night, which usually leads to seeing doubles, and to my amazement sometimes leads to paying doubles. This was the high point of my entire night. My night ended roughly around 3 a.m., I went home and passed out around 5 a.m.

What is it about alcohol that makes you think everyone around you is suddenly deaf? I can always tell when somebody is drunk by hearing them yell across the room about anything that is uninteresting to the person beside them. I myself have been caught in one of these conversations, only to hear it replayed back to me on my ex-boyfriends answering machine a few days later, in which I ATTEMPTED to call him in between breaks of hurling over the toilet next to a complete stranger (male) who happened to be in the same, if not worst, condition as me. Only my conversation sounded flirty and ignorant, remembering why I chose to go this route while being recorded, I couldn't even recall what this guy looked like, only that he had two heads, dark hair, and eyes. He must've had eyes. That was the third time I had gotten drunk in my life and not the last that I regretted doing so, which is why you would think I would be so understanding while waiting on drunk people until 3 a.m., but I'm not. It's annoying and I only want you to talk really loud beside me if I'm drunk too.

Speaking of drinking, it's not only limited to weekends. When you work in a bar, you get the privilege of experiencing intoxicated people all the time. During the weeknights, we have a different drink special for each day of the week. On Wednesday, we have ladies' night. Ladies night consists of $5 martinis (normally $9) and with the purchase of a drink, you can get a half-price appetizer. Weeknights are always more manageable than weekend shifts because the volume of people aren't as high but that doesn't short you on rude people. I work every Wednesday night, YAY! I usually get groups or pairs of chill females, looking for a cheap night out with the girls. Sometimes, I just get the cheap. I approached my third table of the night; it's the same as all my other tables that night, two females looking for some martinis and half-off appetizers. This doesn't make you cheap. Everybody wants a good deal. One of the ladies, probably in her later 30s, ordered a key lime martini and her friend, around the same age, ordered a Pomtini. They then ordered four appetizers. I politely let them know that our special was as I had mentioned before, one alcoholic drink for one half-off appetizer, two drinks for two half-off, and so on. They looked at me rudely, as if to say we understand that, as if to say I assumed they were cheap. I did. I assured them I wasn't being rude and that some people were confused about the special (I don't know why people were confused). Ten minutes after their food had arrived, I got my first complaint. One of the ladies did not like her drink. Every restaurant and bar have different policies surrounding sending a drink back. I personally don't think it should be allowed. I for one have never sent a drink back. I may have not liked a drink, but I will down it and quickly order a different one if this occurs. I do remember once taking a chocolate martini as a shot because it was so gross. It was an awful idea, but at least I didn't send it back. It was not the bartender's fault I ordered something that I had no idea if I would like it in the first place, and it wasn't my fault that somehow the lady at my table forgot that she didn't like lime when ordering a key lime martini. I mean if I didn't know I liked salt and then decided to try a salty pretzel, and then remembered why I didn't like salt in the first place, I shouldn't be allowed to regurgitate my pretzel and give it back to the person who served it to me. I should stop ordering salt, but our policy allowed you to send it back. She sent it back, along with the three other drinks she would go on to order. By the fourth martini, I went to my manager to tell him that if she sent one more thing back, I would lose it. He didn't think the situation was bad enough to approach the table until EVERYTHING started getting sent back, including things that had been sitting on the table for at least thirty minutes. Suddenly, her friend didn't like her drink that she had been sipping on for at least a half an hour and they let me know that our desserts were awful. After the desserts were sent back, my manager had to go up to them. He told them perhaps this wasn't the place for them and that obviously our menu was not agreeing with them. He came back and told me they were polite, and he would take care of their desserts for them (are you kidding me?). I found the whole situation more amusing than anything and kept a smile on my face the entire time. I knew they were only putting on a show for my manager in hopes to have a low bill, and I couldn't wait to give them their bill with their full price appetizers still attached (despite the special we were running). Not minutes after dropping off their check did, she say something about her appetizers not being discounted, I was more than happy to remind her of what our special was, as I had stated in the beginning. "Ma'am, just because you ordered four drinks does not mean you get four half-off appetizers, especially if you send all of your drinks back and expect to not be charged for them, see the deal only works with a PURCHASE of an alcoholic drink." She impolitely wrote: NO TIP in the tip line of her credit card receipt. I'm glad she somehow reasoned with her conscious that this was my fault. I mean it's not like I went out of my way to lay out the specifications of the special as soon as they sat down or anything. I took it with a grain of salt and approached my next table. The rest of the night went fine, but you would be surprised how one bad table can outweigh your entire night of good tables. I must have repeated this unimportant story to my co-workers the rest of the night, mostly for their entertainment and mine, when finally a co-worker who was not amused from working a double and had not made any money let me know that my story was insignificant and that it was just a tip. Just a tip rang in my head...it wasn't just a tip. I almost let him in on how I lost my virginity with almost the same line but thought he would also find that insignificant. Sure, I would have other tips the rest of the night and rest of my life, but I had wasted my time on that one. Nobody says, "It's just a tip," if it's a good tip. I ignored him; he was grumpy and unpleasant, which I could have completely related to in the past, when I worked plenty of unsatisfying doubles. Now I refused to work before four p.m. He would learn this with time, that working nights is the only way to go in a restaurant. The rest of the week went as all the other weeks had went. A few good customers that don't make for interesting stories and a few more bad people that went as follows: 1.) A guy who asked if next time I could make sure liquor was in his alcoholic drink. I assured him we didn't forget the first time, and when I returned to the table with his second round of drinks, he said that his wife said he was being rude. He then asked me if he was. The question alone seemed rude; I told him that I really don't think there was a nice way to tell somebody that you thought they had been ripping you off. We both laughed, him because he thought I was joking, and me because I wasn't joking and just got away with telling him that he was a jerk. 2.) Two women didn't like our wings. They weren't well done enough. I asked them if I could get them something else instead or perhaps have them cooked longer to their liking. They refused my help, but when the bill came, they were appalled that I had charged them for the wings. "Are you seriously charging us for these wings?" I stared down at their empty plates where only bones and a ramekin of blue cheese dressing laid and where I would usually sugar coat a reason why or why not it was something we could fix. I instead said, "Yes, I am charging you for the wings you ate, but I will get my manager." I knew that he would make me look stupid by taking off their awful wings after I told them no, but I didn't care. He did take them off, because they obviously went through a lot of shit eating every single one of those awful uncooked wings, surprisingly where a tip would not be seen after an incident like this. They still tipped me decent or maybe they had extra money to tip me only after we took off the wings from their bill and those are how my shifts go on and off for a while, some decent people and then some complete shit.

JUST THE TIP

CHAPTER SIXTEEN
SOMETIMES WE HAVE TO DEAL WITH A LOT OF SHIT!

Literally. It's not unlikely on a weekend to find some pretty disgusting objects left throughout the bar and in the bathrooms at 3 a.m. Throw-up is not just limited to toilets and urinals these days, but can pop up in hidden corners or under the bar as well. To me, this isn't the strange part. The strange part is that after these incidents happen, nobody feels the need to tell somebody on staff about it. We just must wait until the smell of three-hour-old vomit that was left on the dance floor makes its way on somebody's high heels that happens to be stomping past us on their way to the bathroom. "What is that awful smell? Body odor? Vomit? Fish and chips?" Usually a combination of all three. Sometimes I have even found underwear in the bathroom. With all of the things I have left at a bar, my underwear never made it on the list. One time, we found underwear in the guy's bathroom, shoved in a corner with feces in them. Hopefully, the feces and the underwear both belonged to the same owner. Most of the time, we link this kind of behavior to alcohol, which we only accept because it puts money in our pockets, but somehow the money is never enough to clean up people's "crap" all the time. One time while on my way to the bathroom to put my hair up into a ponytail before my night shift, the day hostess told me that a lady had come in around lunch time to use the bathroom. The lady had then smeared her own feces on the toilet lid, the walls, and the stall door handle as she left. I'm sure the main door to the bathroom was also touched and the door to leave and enter the building as well, but this was not mentioned in the story. Our manager had gotten a complaint saying that the bathroom smelled awful. After having the hostess check out the bathroom, she discovered that some shit had went down. Our manager ended up having to point out the lady who had left her artwork all over the bathroom in a line up at a police station later on in the day after the cops had arrested a few women that fit the hostess's description of her. I made a mental note never to use our bathrooms again, especially the first stall as long as I was employed here. I couldn't help but think to myself how the cops even knew who to arrest for that lineup. Was it the human feces on her hands that gave it away? Was it that she smelled like cow manure? Who were the other innocent girls in the lineup with her? What resemblance did they have with each other? Is it a crime to smell bad? I guess in this case it was. I told the hostess that I was sorry she had such a shitty day and clocked in for my shift. I think there is going to be a day when I am sitting on my couch, thinking back to the days when I worked in the restaurant industry, and shake my head and laugh. Thinking about these stories now, still make me laugh in disbelief.

Speaking of stories involving bathrooms, I bet you have never watched a guy get completely wasted at 2 pm in the afternoon on a Monday at your place of employment. I did, but that was the normal part. After one of my customers decided to drink his woes away for hours, he had to do what any drunk person has to do constantly while drinking, he had to urinate. Okay, I know what you are thinking, not a big deal! Hey, we have all broken the seal. However, instead of him walking towards the bathroom where most people felt the need to handle this situation, he instead arose out of his seat that took entirely too long for any capable, healthy person to do so, and turned to the guy beside him to lean on his shoulder. I think this was more so to help him balance himself so that he would not hit his face on our wooden floors. He rested his right hand on this stranger's shoulder while his left hand unbuttoned his jeans and when I thought it couldn't be anymore strange for the random guy beside him, he did the unthinkable. He started urinating on the man beside him. The man who didn't know him was very furious and got up, which obviously left the unbalanced pissing man to fall to the ground where he finished urinating on himself and the bar as if the bar was his open range urinal. We obviously kicked him out immediately, and I never saw him again. I just can't help but think what the random guy went home thinking or feeling. I bet he never thought that would happen to him in his entire life, and I wonder how many times he has told the story about how he was once in a bar having a beer, but after a while, he realized the man beside him had been pissing on his leg. Oh, alcohol, you may be the sole reason I am able to have these ridiculous stories from people, so thank you.

CHAPTER SEVENTEEN
YOUR SERVER
IS A DRUG ADDICT

What? Like you didn't already think that? I didn't say illegal drug addict, although you should never rule this out either. There are plenty of drugs that we NEED to have throughout our shifts just to stay afloat. In fact, for two dollars, the bartenders provided us with cocaine, I mean red bull. Then there's Adderall itself. This is usually not free, but that really depends on your dealer. Did you know every server I have ever worked with was diagnosed with A.D.D. or maybe it was every server I knew took Adderall, I can't remember now. Personally, I have never been diagnosed with A.D.D. but am 100% sure I suffer from it. I just know I don't have to go to a doctor, who I won't be paying attention to anyways, to tell me that I have a hard time paying attention. We carry candy in our aprons in case we need a sugar high, have access to unlimited shots of soda throughout the night, and there is an espresso machine in our reach at all times, so it's pretty safe to say that your server is on something. Servers are the main reason why Red Bull and Starbucks stay in business; they are basically our drug dealers. With them, they make our shifts seem manageable. I know, here I go again on a waitress rant, "Life is hard" etc. I am fully aware that a lot of jobs are harder than that of a server, the only difference being at every other job, you get paid for, wait for it, for showing up. Imagine showing up to work every day, hoping that you weren't getting a pay cut. Imagine having to comprehend somebody telling you that they can't tip you because the economy is bad or that they aren't paying their bill because they are homeless, and they will be waiting across the street to be arrested in hopes they won't have to sleep outside tonight, so you purposely don't want to call the cops. Imagine working in a restaurant in the south that didn't serve honey mustard! Imagine not having to imagine any of this because you see it every day, and now imagine the unimaginable, having to be sober while doing it. Yeah, I thought you would start to understand. Some people don't like that their server is high, and we don't like that some people are high maintenance. Did you know that around eighty percent of servers go straight to the bar after a shift and give their money right back to their place of employment? The service industry ranks in the top ten for most depressing jobs, one poll had even put servers as high as number 3 for most depressing jobs, only behind childcare and in-home nursing care. The only reason I think they the other two occupations beat us is because they have more physical contact with customers and uncontrollable bodily liquids are involved that can't be blamed on alcohol. I'm just giving you reasons to give your server an easier time if their eyes seem more squinty than usual or if they forget your order before making it back to the computer to put it in.

JUST THE TIP

CHAPTER EIGHTEEN
WE ARE ALL ACTORS, ACTING LIKE SERVERS

Everybody wonders why all waiters and waitresses think they can be actors and actresses. How can you blame us? We have the best experience tips can buy. We have to act every single day when we go to work. We act like we are doing good when were not, we act like we care that you don't have ranch to dip your fries in before your food hits the table, and we act like it doesn't bother us to hand back your change you asked for even when its 45 cents. You couldn't tell me the same waitress who politely picked up your credit card receipt in which you left no tip wasn't the same waitress who hoped you left your credit card or phone behind which she would accidently misplace forever.

One time, I had a guy sit at one of my tables for hours on his iPad, not only did he take up my table for hours, he also didn't tip me. He left his iPad on the table when he left. I was quite surprised for this exchange; it was more than I was expecting. He didn't have to do that. Unfortunately, he came back. I pulled his iPad from the kitchen where I had placed it and wondered what kind of fight, he would actually put up for it. I handed it back to him with a smile on my face; this was his second opportunity to tip me. He said, "Thanks," and started to walk away. I murmured under my breath, "Thanks for not tipping me and being a complete self-centered douche bag."

"Excuse me?" he asked.

Oh, my gosh! Did I just say that out loud? Probably not too loud... "You're welcome! You also forgot your iPad carrier bag."

Some situations are harder to act in than others. One slow Thursday night, as usual, I was counting down the hours until I could go home and do nothing. I never thought of the irony of this until just now, wanting to leave doing nothing so bad just to do nothing in a different location, and more than likely in a different position. With about an hour to go and no hopes of the second coming happening anytime soon, a table of ten came in. Normally, ten people would light up my eyes. Money and gratuity would dance around my head like sugar plums, but my bubbles were shortly popped when between all ten of the young, loud, obnoxious people that had just walked in, they had ordered two chicken finger meals, all waters except for three sodas between, and they had a lot of time to loiter in my section. Not only was this table not worth adding gratuity, but I also knew I wasn't getting tipped when three of them asked me how much, with tax included, would a side of fries be. When I told one of the guys that the side of fries was an even three dollars, he looked dumbfounded. It was probably because he had already ordered the side without asking the price first, and I could see the idea of him running out on me when the bill came bouncing around in his head. I was just hoping he had enough money for his food, I would take a loss on my tip. I think, when all was said and done, I received a total of three dollars in tips from the table of ten. Not only did I not get tipped but money would come out of my pocket on the sales from them. You must tip out the hostess and bartender a certain amount, depending on your sales that night. Thankful they were done and ready for them and myself to leave, I noticed everybody hanging out and frantically looking for one of the lady's purses, even though lady is hardly the term I would use when describing this particular female. They asked if I had seen her purse, and I told them I had not but would keep my eyes open. I didn't think it was a big deal because people left things at the bar all the time. Most of the time, it usually turned up. I also couldn't figure out why she was freaking out, when she obviously had not had enough money to tip me, so I assumed her purse and wallet were empty. After about ten minutes of going back and forth between the bathroom and the bar, they started giving me dirty looks and talking about me in front of my face.

"I think she took it," was a phrase that started getting thrown around. They then asked the bartender if I was the only female working that night (I was) and said they were sure they had left it in the bathroom. I almost lost my shit. Not only for the third time did these people not tip me, but now I stole their purse. The bartender asked me to check the bathroom which I loudly declined, thinking it would only be my luck to find the purse of somebody as rude and as stupid as that. I rolled my eyes at them and was mentally preparing to swing a fist. It's true; I don't know how to fight, which has always been a weakness of mine, considering my strength has always been being able to piss people off. Right then, three of the women started yelling at me, saying that I stole the friend's purse. One of these women actually then came over to me to ask me if I could charge her phone! I told her she shouldn't leave it near me because I might steal it. I then pointed out that none of them tipped me, in case they had forgotten. This is usually a no-no. At this point, I was pretty sure so was accusing your untipped waitress of stealing your purse. They threatened to call the cops and I told the bartender that if he didn't beat them to it, that I would. I didn't make enough money tonight to deal with half the conversation I had just encountered. They even went as far as to ask the bouncer, someone in which they confided in, to check the back dumpster. "NO! Don't go back there! That's where I hide all my stolen purses!"

I couldn't take it anymore. I started laughing hysterically, wondering what reality show my coworkers had put me on. I looked up and around, then into the mirrors in the bar, where were the cameras? Where was Ashton? The cameras never revealed themselves, and Ashton never came running out of the dry pantry. This only meant one thing. This was real life; this was my life, as a server. The woman found her purse in her car hours later, (this is only what I imagined happening) and I went home broke and disappointed that the episode I had just witnessed would never make its way to television. I always thought servers would make for an interesting reality show. Servers are good actors; after all, I woke up the next morning and acted like nothing happened the night before. A day doesn't go by that I don't refer to my Acting for Dummies book right before a shift after I read my Servers are Dummies book, of course.

JUST THE TIP

CHAPTER NINETEEN
GROUPON: HELPING SERVERS GET SCREWED SINCE 2008

Nothing is more romantic then when you are giving a table their check, and they pull out their iPhone and say, "I have something for you." An iPhone makes for an excellent tip by the way, especially to a waitress such as me, who has lost her iPhone and finds out it is five hundred dollars to replace it. "Oh, my gosh! Thank you so much!" I take the iPhone from his hand and just as I am about to walk off, the guy grabs my hand, slowly and firm. I have butterflies even though his family is sitting right there. "We have a Groupon," He said. My heart broke: how could he do this to me!?

Every time somebody hands me a Groupon at the end of their bill, it nearly cuts their bill of purchased drinks and food in half. Most deals with Groupon allow for an automatic gratuity, but sometimes our managers forget to add the gratuity, and contrary to belief, we do not have the power to add gratuity because you hold the potential of possibly sucking. This particular table had a fifty-dollar tab. I tell the guy who is in his mid-50s that I will need to take his phone to the back, to scan the bar code. He looks at me as if I'm the one being shady. HELLO!! I am not the one who is trying to make half of my bill disappear!

He gives me his phone, and I always make some sort of joke to let my tables know that I am not openly stealing their phone.

"If I'm not back in 10 minutes, you know where I work," I say.

They hardly ever smile or laugh at this, which makes me think this country lacks trust all together or that I need new material. After going to my manager to tell him I have a Groupon, I notice this particular couple's bill goes from fifty dollars to twenty-five after the manager punches in some number code that has the ability to decide if I will fall short on my own cell phone bill. I don't see the total of the bill dropping, all I see is my tip being cut in half. What did I ever do to Groupon? I give the table back their check and walk away hoping they leave a tip based on the original amount.

"Ma'am, our phone??"

"Oh, yes." I take their phone from my apron and hand it to them. I almost feel like using it for collateral for a decent tip, even though I'm told this is illegal.

They sit outside on the patio for a while until I forget they are there. My bar gets busy and my attention is on other guests. I finally make my way outside to their table to see that they left me a three-dollar tip. I look at this as a three-dollar tip on a fifty-dollar bill. I gave them great service. Did they think if they sat there long enough, I would forget what their original tab was? Unfortunately, memory loss isn't one of my flaws. I know what you may be thinking. Boy, is money all waitstaff care about? Are waitstaff just self-absorbed and money-grabbing? Well, for the most part, the industry is full of these. My intention is not to make you think you have to tip well. We work hard for tips, and it's how we pay our bills. I'm just letting you know what is expected if you happened to be me standing on the other side of the table. You can't blame me for always expecting big tips. Most of the time, I'm disappointed. Size does matter.

CHAPTER TWENTY
PEOPLE ARE ASSHOLES

It is a Tuesday night, and due to my awesome work schedule, I had the pleasure of having the last three days off. My three days off were awesome. I didn't do anything of any real significance, but I didn't have to wait on people and that makes it great without reason. I'm usually ready to come back to work on Tuesday, due to the fact that I spent three whole days not doing anything, and that the nothing I did cost me all of the money in my wallet. I go into work in a pretty good mood. I'm always greeted with a lot of "hellos" since people haven't seen me in a few days. Unfortunately, they have been stuck working endless doubles. I look very refreshed compared to them.

I get my first table around 5:30, shortly after arriving at 5 pm. It's three regulars I have become very familiar with because they have been coming in for the last two years I have been employed here. They work across the street at the courthouse and at least show up for a drink three times a week. They are always pleasant and easy to deal with. I wish all my tables were like them. After a while, a few more couples come in for dinner and drinks. I'm wondering why nobody is sitting outside; it's so nice outside!!!!! As soon as I think this, I'm told I have a party of ten outside. Damn. I spoke too soon. I go outside to greet my ten top. I'm glad I'm getting tables because I may be able to pay all my bills if this consistency stays up like this for the next ten days.

"Hi, how are you guys doing today?" In a strong German accent, I heard, "We will take eight Pauleners, good German beer." I try to make a joke about how we may run out if they keep ordering the Pauleners. They didn't find it funny. In fact, I felt completely awkward every time I went to their table. Eventually, we did run out of Paulener beers. They also didn't find that funny. They were a little needy, but had a good tab with gratuity, so I couldn't complain. While I was focusing on getting the Germans their beer, my whole side of the patio filled up, which consisted of six tables. One table crosses my mind. The hostess seats me with a single dark-skinned young guy with bright blue contacts and a fedora hat at a table made for six, even though he is by himself. Something is off about him right away. Maybe it's his contacts, he looks like Michael Jackson from thriller only his contacts are avatar blue instead of baby puke yellow. He puts his order in with the hostess, and she tells me he seems pissed that she took a while to get to him in the first place. I notice how needy he is when I'm waiting on him. He orders some wine, an appetizer, and a burger. He then starts ordering rounds of champagne for him and a new friend who has suspiciously joined him. His friend looks homeless. I can say that because there is a good chance that he was homeless, if you have ever been to Fayetteville Street in Raleigh. A lot of people like to make this street their home in between homes. The fact that they were drinking champagne even made the whole situation more bizarre to me. They were both assholes. When I wasn't at their table, they were calling me away from my other tables to ask stupid questions, but instead of calling me by my name or with words, they would whistle, as if I was their pet dog and they were trying to call me back home after realizing I had strayed too far. I had a bad feeling about them and told the hostess I thought they were going to walk out on their tab. I went inside to grab another table's drink order and when I got back, I noticed the guys were not at the table. My heart rate went up as I knew they had just walked out on their tab, only to see avatar return to get his phone that he left on the table.

"If you leave the table, I will need a credit card."

"Oh, we aren't leaving." Sure, you're not. I trust you completely. I go inside and tell the hostess to go outside and see if he leaves the table until I get back. Not two seconds later, they both start walking down the street with their champagne and round the corner of the next block. HELL, NO! I take off at a full speed sprint, thinking to myself that my new Nikes I had just bought a few days prior felt great for running and suddenly made me appreciate the hundred dollars that they had cost me. As soon as I rounded the corner I saw them, just walking and talking, with champagne in hand as if it was no big deal that they were a) drinking on a public street and b) they had no sense of urgency for just bailing on a seventy dollar tab. I grab the guy by the arm and tell him he needs to come with me and pay his fucking tab. His face turns to shock; he can't believe I ran after them. "Ah, CHILL OUT, GIRL, we weren't trying to leave, we were just getting cigarettes."

"Yeah, whatever."

One of the guys jokes about how I am a fast runner and goes in for a hug saying, "Don't worry, we wouldn't do that to you."

"Fuck you." One of the guys has the nerve to comment on his race being a key factor in me running after them.

"No, the key factor is I told you not to leave without giving me a card and you did." They come back to sit at their table, and I want them to pay immediately and get off of our property. They already broke at least two laws, and I want to call the cops. My manager wants me to give them the benefit of the doubt as I beg him to go out there and get them to pay. Not ten minutes after they finish their champagne, they take off running through an alley behind the courthouse located in front of my work. This time, I don't even bother. I don't know what else is waiting for me in the alley, but I'm guessing its more homeless people who are assholes and don't tip. Usually when a table walks out on their tab, you are responsible for paying it out of your pocket. His tab was seventy dollars that I refused to pay. My boss ended up comping it off because I had let him know that they had already walked out and would probably do it again before the night was over. I'm frustrated because I think it could have been prevented, and I wasted three hours of my life waiting on two guys who didn't tip me. I try to push my luck and ask my boss if he can somehow give me a twenty percent tip on their bill, due to the fact I had to run after them and reminded him that running wasn't a part of our job description and that he was lucky to have a past track runner on his team of employees. He didn't give me a tip, so I gave him one: "Next time I tell you a guy walked out on his tab and is now back, after I chased him down, can we please make them leave immediately after paying with an automatic gratuity. Thank you." If any of you see this guy, please contact me so I can officially kick his skinny ass. Thanks, from all his future waitresses of Raleigh. I leave work that night mad, mad at myself, mad at my boss, mad that people can be such assholes. I think about this while lying in bed. I almost felt like a cop who caught two criminals who later escaped. I almost was badass. I put it out of my mind, took my loss and fell asleep. Nobody should spend this much time thinking about people they don't know.

I wake up excited for a new day, and even though I know I must work later, I put it out of my mind since its still hours away. I go to the gym and do my monthly workout. I run two miles and do some old school crunches. I know everybody says they don't work, and I have yet to see results, but I am too lazy to memorize the countless shapes in magazine workouts stacked under my bed. I really should do that soon. Then I go to the pool, hoping I can tan anything the gym may have missed, finally shower and then head to work.

I must go in early for a sixty top, which is awesome because it's an automatic gratuity in which everybody is on one tab which makes it that much easier for me. They aren't needy or rude and they basically have to beg me to let them spend more of their bosses' money. They only stay for about three hours and then leave. This shift couldn't have started any better. The rest of the shift stays consistent. I literally have not stopped to even get a drink of water since three-thirty in the afternoon. It is now midnight, and I am damn right exhausted. Unfortunately, we are open until two a.m. tonight, and although I love the consistency of the tips I am receiving, my feet and back are arguing with me that I need to sit down, maybe have a drink and eat, since the last time I stopped to refuel was ten hours ago. I agree and do just that. Right then a ten top walks in. Here is a trick in waitressing. If you ever want an abundant number of tables to come in, instead of posting your specials all over social media sites, have your waitstaff order their dinner. I have never seen so many people decide to come into one place as I do when my dinner has just come up in the window. I don't know about anybody else, but the last thing I want to do when I'm hungry is to give other people their food, while mine sits in the window getting cold, even though I'm only paying three dollars less than the average customer for it. I know. It's my fault for trying to eat on the clock, but let me remind you, it has been ten hours that I have now been on my shift, and I am not legally obliged to have a break. So, yeah. A ten top walks in. Great. I go up to them and grab their drink orders, even though some of them already have drinks. Usually, this bothers me because people who open multiple tabs usually only remember one of them, but I'm too tired to babysit tonight. I bring them their drinks; they seem friendly enough, and they order a bunch of appetizers. I hurry up and try to eat my own food in between making sure that stuffing their own faces is going well. Everything seems to check out. They are my last table of the night, so I wait in the bar for them to ask for their check, while occasionally approaching them asking if everything is still okay, meaning: Are you done yet? Finally, I see a few people go to the bar, to get their bar tab and leave. Three of them didn't pay me for their food so I assume it's on their friend's tab who is an older couple still sitting at the table. The couple finally asks me for their bill. I have a bad feeling about it because people have let me down lately, more so this week in particular. A few moments later, I heard, "Ma'am. We only got a few appetizers, not all of this stuff."

"I know. Everybody at the table just left and didn't pay me," I reply in an undermining tone.

"NO, they wouldn't do that. They are the most trustworthy people we know, trust us." Maybe you should get some more trustworthy friends. I tell them that I'm sure their friends probably didn't mean to walk out on their food and that I wasn't accusing them of being bad people, but that they only seemed to pay their bar tab and not their food tab—by accident, of course. The couple went back and forth with me trying to convince me that I was being shady and double charged them for what their friends had already paid for. I assured them I wasn't but told them that they should call their good friends and have them come back to pay their food. They never called them. I don't think they even had their numbers but had met them at a concert prior that was being held at the end of the street. I then let them know that double charging them for food in no way helped me out whatsoever, that I didn't get a cut on profits made on food or drinks but only tips. They then kept saying they weren't the type of people to get mad while continuously getting angrier and angrier with me. I could tell they weren't listening to a word I said, I felt like a broken record and refused to repeat myself anymore. I then went and took off their gratuity, that I rightfully earned, the policy on a table of any more than six people. I gave them back their check and let them know that usually we do put a gratuity on a party of their size. The guy still angrily murmurs under his breath, "Yeah, I saw that."

I interrupt him before he said something that he would soon regret. "Well, I took that off for you, sir."

"What? No, you don't have to do that."

Of course, I do, or you will complain more, is what I felt like saying.

"Yes, I feel bad you have to pay for food that isn't yours, just make sure you check with your friends when you see them again and you will see that it was just an honest mistake."

I just count that table as a loss and am so glad my night is finally over with. I go to the table to collect the signed copy of their tab. They leave the same tip as if the gratuity was still on it. I am in shock, but not because they were decent enough to recognize the fact that I was just doing my job, but on the bottom of the receipt read a comment: "I'm a photographer. Shoot with me sometime." Wow. That just happened. I was surprised and grossed out. The number on the bottom was scratched out but still readable. I'm guessing his female friend, which was more than likely his wife, was responsible for ruining his graffiti on my credit card slip that I needed to turn into my boss. It was the second night in a row, in a long time that I had to deal with assholes. I was hoping this was not going to become a routine, but I'd been in the business long enough to know better.

CHAPTER TWENTY-ONE
STUCK SOMEWHERE BETWEEN NOT MAKING ANY MONEY AND NOT WANTING ANY CUSTOMERS TO COME IN

While serving, it's almost like you have to trick yourself into forgetting that you are, in fact, serving. It's a Tuesday night. Surprisingly, the weekdays for me are usually good, better than some weekend nights in fact. I work all the weeknight shifts, it's my secret at this particular establishment. This Tuesday doesn't seem to be as promising as the others before it. I engage in conversation with three of my coworkers who happen to all be on doubles. They tell me they have only averaged thirty dollars for their morning shift— thirty dollars between all three of them. OUCH! For some reason when lunch is dead, you expect the same flow of traffic to continue throughout the entire day and night. Tonight, was the perfect example. After an hour or so, after arriving at 5, I get my first table. A guy in his later 30s, completely bald, with a baby blue dress shirt on. He's on the phone.

"Would you like a menu?" I ask him. He nods yes. I give him time to finish his phone call. I check up on him three more times to see if he is ready to order, and he gives me the finger. The index fingers. I hate when people put their first finger in my face. I decide to not come back until his obviously very important phone call is over with, but I don't get a chance to go back, as soon as he gets off the phone, he goes up to the bartender to place an order. The bartender comes up to me after I watch this transaction take place and says, "Your guy is ready to order."

Cool. He can wait a minute, as I have waited several for him to finish his phone call. That is the nature of my job, waiting, yet it's something I can never get used to. He's in and out really quick and leaves me a five-dollar tip. My next table won't arrive for another hour. When you haven't had any human interaction with a customer in over an hour, you want to write off your entire shift and be done with it. This whole night went like that: totaling in five tables for my seven-hour shift. I made $25 with no hourly paycheck to make up for my loss. I almost go to the bar to get a drink but realize I really don't have the funds at this particular time and spending everything I made that night on liquids that I would piss out by morning seemed more like a junkie decision than a smart one.

The next night goes the same way. It's two hours in and nobody has sat at a table. A few stragglers at the bar and a staff not getting paid to stand around and catch up on previous weekend plans. Two hours into my shift and the dining room servers get cut. You won't believe how good the meaning of being cut sounds when you work in the serving industry. I'm jealous and start praying that by some chance nobody will come in tonight to eat. It's wishful thinking, but for the next hour, it seems possible. I start doing some silverware to occupy my time when I feel a tap on my shoulder.

I know that tap. It is followed by the most annoying words in the universe, "I just sat you two outside."

Not only is there not anybody in the entire restaurant, but now I must go outside to beg for money. I know what you're thinking, I should be happy, I got a table. Unless that table is going to tip me out on the last three hours, I spent not getting paid, it hardly seems worth it, but then again I do have to eat and having someone pay for dinner is always nice. Thank you, customer 1 and 2. Most servers' wants, and needs are very conflicting. We want to make money, we need to make money, we don't want to wait on you, and we don't want you to come in. Some servers are worse than others, but a lot of server's clock in and wait to go home, then love to complain about their lack of funds. In the past, I, too, have been guilty of this. Not now, now I have to stay until midnight, no matter how many customers may or may not come in.

CHAPTER TWENTY-TWO
MORNING WOOD

Have you ever been at a bar as the lights came on at the end of the night? The first thought that goes through my head is: OH, my God. It's already two a.m. I hope I can get food somewhere. Yes, this will be my third dinner for the night, but I'm drunk, so it's okay. My second thought is: this place looked so much better in the dark, and the same goes for the people who are still here. Hey, guy with the gold teeth, please stop talking to me. They only looked cool when the bar was still dark, and the black lights were reflecting on them. I thought you had a fucking rainbow shooting out of your mouth for God's sake, so of course I was impressed! It's almost like bars shouldn't exist past a certain time. They only make sense at night after a ton of alcohol has been consumed. I think one of the most depressing places in the world to be is at a bar, in the morning. This brings me to my next point: I was finally promoted to a bartender. A daytime bartender. The worst.

There is nothing worse than walking into a bar that is recovering from a weekend night. The bar still reeks of Bud Light and liquor stains on the wooden floors that have been mopped over twice, yet you can still tell that the water that was used to mop smells of mildew from the night before. I'm pretty sure I remember somebody throwing up on the carpet in that corner last night. I go to look. It has been cleaned up, but now the carpet there is a different color than the rest. I'm sure nobody will be able to tell. I pull one of the dining room chairs over it to fix the problem. You know some things right off the bat about your morning bartender: one is, they are new, or they would have never agreed to work such a pathetic shift that really only requires you to clean and make sure the night bartender, who will make triple what you make, is ready for his or her shift. Also, your bartender might potentially be hung over. There is a good chance that he or she is. So be nice. You are sitting at a bar and it is only 11 a.m., after all.

At this bar, the floors and entire bar are made of wood. At night, the red lights lining the bar give the wooden floor and bar a glow of warmth, something that has become very comforting to me in my years of working at this particular establishment, but during the day, the floors lack shine and look dirty. The bar looks like a giant chunk of wood with a marble slab placed on top. My opening duties are to turn the lights on, clean the bar top, stock beer, stock beer, and stock more beer. I may have a few business guys in for their lunch break, who will not make eye contact or say "hi". They are way too busy to be human during the day. They have to be back in the courtroom within an hour. They will all leave me $2 because apparently that is standard for lunch tipping. I count down the hours until five p.m. hits so that I can run out of here to do the nothing I had planned, but still nothing outside is better than doing the nothing I have been doing inside all day. Of course, we only get paid two dollars and some change an hour, which is not comforting at all when only two tables chose to be in your presence that day.

Now on a Sunday, things are different. It is totally acceptable to go out to a bar at 11 a.m. on a Sunday. There is Sunday football and Sunday brunches to attend. Sunday Funday is now a thing. On a Sunday, I will serve endless mimosas and Bloody Marys made from our homemade Bloody Mary mix that took me an hour to make by mincing up every single vegetable our kitchen had to offer today. Good chance, I will run out of it and won't be able to make more and for that I am sorry. On this Sunday, I decided I wanted to spice things up a bit. Usually our uniform consists of a black T-shirt and jeans, but today I decided to pair my outfit with suspenders that were left the Saturday night before and fake nerdy glasses. Oh, and just to fit every stereotype, I wore my hair in low pigtails. Yes it was cute and nerdy and everything else I was trying to be, but I had no idea it would cause so many people to take time from eating their third plate of macaroni and cheese that was running into their pancakes to comment on it. At no other time during the week is it acceptable to eat macaroni and cheese with pancakes and syrup on the same plate. I love Sundays. I had these five guys come in that were all trying to be cute and flirt with their cute nerdy bartender and usually this annoys me, even though it has no right to. For some reason, today nothing annoyed me, and I played along with them, tried to show them a good time. They were visiting from Pittsburgh and were here for work. Eventually it got to the point of them asking me if I wanted to hang out when I got off work, which I agreed to. Later that night, my roommate and I met up with them at a bar, very few of them were still standing since they had been drinking since noon at my bar for brunch. The two that were standing were super flirty, and after a few drinks, I was okay with that. Fast forward through some drunk making out and waking up in a hotel room later... Okay, I know what you are thinking and NO! The only thing I woke up regretting was the huge hangover that would insist on sharing a cab ride home with me, and the fact that 3 or 4 people were in line for the shower as I laid there with my stupid nerdy outfit still on. Somehow that was more embarrassing than waking up with nothing on at all. I walked down to the lobby with one of the guys and walked outside to grab a cab, only to notice, there were none. Not trying to stand in one place with my outfit choice, I decided to walk home. It was only a few blocks, but it was freezing outside. This sucks. I should stop drinking, were my thoughts as I went through the homeless park and passed the train tracks. Just as I'm walking up the driveway, my roommate is coming out the door to go to work. We just exchanged looks, and she gets in her car laughing. I couldn't help but laugh either, my excursions after my break-up always ended up funny. None of the pieces fit for a while, and I was also okay with that.

The guys would text me here and there if they were going to be back on business, but I usually never wrote back. The one time I did, I got a reply a few moments later saying the guy who had texted me was engaged and his fiancé was very upset I had texted her man. I was so confused. This guy had just texted me to ask me what I was doing. Was he in the bathroom when he had texted me?? That was such a quick turnaround rate. Oh, and then him being engaged was something he didn't mention! I could have written back and brought up the hotel room, but instead I chose to save his life, the life he obviously cared nothing about and responded, "Congratulations, I wish you guys the best!" Deep down, I felt really sorry for this strange girl who was writing me, because I'm pretty sure she is married now to somebody who hits on nerdy bartenders when he goes away for business. I secretly hope she isn't that dumb and chose to call off the engagement.

I eventually stopped working day bar shifts, mostly because I hated being up that early because people don't make sense to me in the morning. Besides, I eventually retired to night bartender. Now, I'm the person who checks to make sure the day bartender stocked beer, more beer, and even more beer, so that I can make some money for the both of us.

JUST THE TIP

CHAPTER TWENTY-THREE
(TRUE STORIES OF ANNOYING PEOPLE)

As I was in the middle of a dinner rush, I count my tables while I am at the POS putting in another order. By the way POS is a computer system waitresses and waiters use to ring in your food and drink orders. Most servers gave it the nickname 'piece of shit' since it always freezes on you. Somehow, I always think hitting it five million times quickly will help it correct itself. It never does and I look like I'm having convulsions in front of my customers. Okay, so I have nine tables, no big deal, right? All the tables in this bar are lined up evenly in a straight line, which makes it easy to go up and down the line and figure out what people need. I do my occasional water check; table 103 is empty, as well as 105. I make notice and make my way back to the kitchen to get a pitcher to refill both tables with one trip. As I'm walking by one table, I see one of my customers with the empty glass making eye contact with me. Shit. I keep walking by, hoping she doesn't think that I didn't notice her empty water glass. I give her the benefit of the doubt. I only give a few people a night this, don't let me down!

"EXCUSE ME," she calls. "Can I get more water?" I just shake my head and decide no more benefits will be given out tonight, only doubts. I refill table 103 and 105, and as I am walking past my other tables, I notice one needs another Coke. Trying not to make the same mistake as before, I go up to the table to ask them how everything is going and then quickly let them know that I will get them another Coke and ask if there is anything else I can get them.

"Yes, can we get another Coke?"

WHYYYYYYYYYYYYYYYYYYYYYYYYYYYYYYYYYYYY
YYYYYYYYYYYYYYYYYYYYYYYYYYYYYYYYYYYYYYY
YYYYYYYYYYYYYYYYYYYYYYYYYYYYYYYYYYYYYYY
YYYYYYYYYYYYYYYYYYYYYYYYYYYYYYYYYYYYYYY
YYYYYYYYYYYYYYYYYYYYYYYYYYYYYYYYYYYYYYY
YY!!!!!!!!!!!!!!

I know, you're thinking what is the big deal? If you are a server you shared that extended why with me, this happens all the time. Nobody ever listens to what you have to say when you are at their table. I experience that same scene at least three times a night, more on a weekend. One time, I even went up to a girl and was like "Your beer will be right out, the bartenders are just changing the keg."

She nods her head like she understood and as I'm walking away, I hear, "Where's my beer?"

She wasn't the first offender that night so I give it to her straight, "I said it will be right out!"

Sorry that I am being a bitch, but you are customer 10,000 that has done that to me!

~waitress of 7 years and still counting.

It is crazy how many different people you may encounter in one 12-hour shift; it's also that same crazy that out of everybody, they all tell the same jokes. It's not really a joke with a beginning and an ending. It's the same responses to the same questions I ask every night; everybody thinks they are being original and makes the rest of their table laugh. It's also the 5th time that night I heard the same sarcastic response. I no longer can pretend it's funny; I am human after all. Here is an example:

"What kind of beers do you guys have?" a customer asks.

I point to the list that is on the table that was supposed to serve the purpose of him not having to ask me what kind of beers we have. He laughs.

"Oh, it's right in front of me. I will take the Stone IPA."

"Oh, we are out of the stone IPA, but...." He doesn't let me finish, throws his menu up in the air in a playful manner and says, "I guess we have to leave, that's it! Oh no!!!!"

He then looks at his friends to laugh, like he is so funny. I just want to finish telling him the other IPA we replaced it with. I cut him off because this "joke" is going on way too long for a drink order.

"We have Hoptical Illusion IPA instead, would you like that?"

"Sure," he replies. I know this doesn't seem like a big deal, and it's not. It's just one of those things that make you feel like a robot when it happens over and over again, and you are forced to remember how robotic your job really is. Not too long ago I had a lady come up to me and say, "Are you my little waitress? Where is my little waitress?" Something about her calling us "little waitresses" was annoying. I felt like she was not talking about the size of our waist but was belittling us as people. I was not her "little" waitress. I looked nothing like her medium-size waitress.

~waitress who lost her sense of humor

When I go up to a table, I would like for them to look me in the eye when I'm talking to them, so that I can be sure they are listening and understanding me. My biggest pet peeve about serving is when I go up to a table, and they don't respond to a simple question such as, "How are you guys doing today?" Waitresses and waiters are sociable people, but nothing makes us feel more awkward when we are standing at your table staring at the backs of your heads or trying to read your lips that aren't moving. It's the end of the night, and I go up to my table of 6 and ask them if they are doing okay.

"Yes, we are doing good," says ONE of the 6, the rest "can't" see me. I walk away. They immediately go to the bartender to tell him that they have not seen their waitress lately and ask if they can get their checks, all separate, and now they are in a hurry! WHAT?!|?!?! I swear people like to fuck with waitresses and waiters on a daily basis. I refuse to believe they are this stupid.

Everyday my job reminds me of the movie Idiocracy. If you haven't seen it, it's not worth seeing, but the movie is pretty much about a guy who gets put to sleep and wakes up in the future where everybody is a complete idiot. They don't move their trash when they are done eating, they sit on it in their living rooms. They watch TV shows that don't make sense, and they think this guy who shows up who knows how to do basic math and is well trained in traffic laws is a genius. They want to make him president until they get scared, he knows too much. It is idiotic, you get the point.

~waitress who would prefer to be a movie critic

I work at this place that has an outdoor patio to allow guest to eat while enjoying the nice weather outside. This usually helps business in the fall and early spring, other than that it's either too cold or too hot to sit outside. It's not that I don't love the patio; what I don't love is the fact that every place I have ever worked has always placed the patio an inconvenient distance away from the kitchen, and it just so happens, everybody who likes to sit on the patio happens to be the pickiest people I have ever met. We have even put them in a group (patio people). I don't mind going back and forth a few times to get your drinks and your food but please when I ask you if there is anything else you need with your burger, can you not tell me one thing at a time! Recently, I went up to this table and asked them what they would like to drink, they said they weren't ready and asked me to come back, a few minutes later I did, only one person was ready and the other one wanted water. I went and got their drinks and came back just in time for the other one to order her drink. This went on about ten times. Can we get napkins, can we get an ashtray, can we get another ashtray, can we get... Holy shit! I appreciate the exercise, but my shoes suck, and my feet are starting to form blisters. These are not the right shoes for you to suddenly turn into my personal trainer. Yes, I would wear my running shoes if I could, but they aren't all black or slip resistant. You would think with the amount of running I do back and forth, I would be in great shape. Well, I'm not. I have decided that, in order to make some good out of the endless trips I have to take from the back of the restaurant to the front, I will start doing it in sprints so that my heart rate will stay up long enough to burn a few calories, then at the end of my serving career, people will say, "Your legs look awesome. Do you work out?" I will reply, "Not really, I just train them 5 days a week and a minimum of 8 hours a day." Then they will say something like, "That is crazy!" I will agree.

~ waitress who is secretly using her work to train for a marathon

It's 11 p.m., and we close at midnight. The dinner servers were cut at 10 p.m. but the last few tables in the dining room stay and linger, not understanding that their server would like to leave after working since 11 a.m. I must stay until close and am approached by a fellow server asking if I would mind taking over his table. I do mind. They have sat there for hours, they are drunk, and they don't speak English. He tells me he asked them if they would like to cash out with him because he is off, but they say they would rather be transferred, and they have an over 100-dollar tab. What a bunch of dicks. He reluctantly gives me the table and a potential $20 tip. After approaching the table, they ask me for four Jager bombs. I like the fact that they are adding to their bill in hopes it will add to my tip. It seems the only English they know is Jager and bombs. I'm glad they are choosing to use these words together. It's almost midnight, and I tell them we are about to do last call. They order their fourth round of shots and ask for the bill. I'm considering adding gratuity, they have been sitting there for five hours. I can't add gratuity because our policy is six or more, and there are only four of them. They seem friendly enough. I give them their check and wait. It reaches around 12:40, and they are still here. I'm becoming very impatient that I have to stay an extra hour for this one table, but know on a $200- tab, I should walk away with an extra forty dollars. They finally leave around 1 a.m. I pick up their check and start cussing out loud. They were lucky they were gone or I know I would have said something to lose my job. I go and complain to the bartender and even call the manager who was on duty earlier to let him know the status of the table that he told me not to gratuity. He says he is sorry and offers to buy me dinner sometime (He never does). I look down on the receipt one more time and wonder what kind of people can stay somewhere for five hours and tip me $2 dollars on $200!!!!! I received no tip for this table but will have to tip out 3% of the extra 200 in sales they racked up on my server report. I put zero in because 2 dollars is somehow more offensive. I give them the benefit of the doubt and instead of ruling them out as assholes, I blame it on the fact that they aren't from here. We all do that. "They don't know any better. Over there, the waitresses get paid hourly."

I'm sick of making excuses for people who live on the other side of the ocean and know that they are completely capable of

Googling our tipping policies.
~waitress who plans on moving to "over there"

EPILOGUE
CLOSING ARGUMENTS

When I first began serving, nobody could have told me it would be an ongoing career choice for ten years and counting. I'm glad I didn't know at the time because my life would have gone in the exact same direction had I known otherwise and that would have been sad. Whether I like it or not, waitressing is the reason why I am the way I am today. I will forever have a unique outlook on people. Sometimes I will notice while sitting at a bar with a drink in hand, the guy who is out with his "boys" ordering 10 shots and "getting the tab" but forgetting to "get the tip." I will observe people while waiting on my own food to come to the table at a sit down restaurant, where I notice the couple in front of me is not happy, not enjoying their meal out together, but find common interest in treating their waitress like shit. After all, they will probably never see her again and social skills are not required when people will not remember you. Here is a tip: If you are a shitty customer and come back to the same place thinking your waitress will not remember you, just know, we always remember.

Being a waitress has taught me many life skills, which in my opinion makes me an awesome person. I will list them now in no order of awesomeness:

- Learning how to carry three plates at one time (my boyfriend loves that I can bring them their drink, dinner, and a snack all at the same time) multiple trips to the kitchen suck!

- Learning that duck, beef, and some pork are cooked to temp. I will never have to be embarrassed like so many others while eating out when my waitress asks, "How would you like your duck cooked?" All my friends with "grown-up" jobs will be in shock that I ordered the duck but then, "I'll take the duck medium, please." They all smile with ease. "She's pretty smart for a waitress," they all say.

- Knowing exactly what drinks to get and not get in order to get drunk. I go out with my friends, "What's on special?" they ask the bartender. "Four-dollar vodka." "I'll take a vodka cranberry. Tonya, would you like one?" "No. I don't feel like cranberry juice right now, I feel like getting drunk. I will take 2 shots of captain and some coke to chase it with." "That's so expensive, $14, Tonya?" "Yes, let me know how much you end up spending on vodka cranberry's, we will compare bills and drunkenness later."

- I know not to go out to eat unless you are having a "cheat day" because even the salads at most any restaurants have more calories than your daily intake.

- I will always have an endless cash flow in my wallet, who needs a bank account?!

Okay, so maybe not as many promising qualities as I thought. The point being, you only become this well rounded of a person after spending endless nights until 3 am delivering people fries and beer. It is a lost art that will probably never be known in its entirety. Without serving, I would have never met any of my boyfriends and look how well they all worked out. My whole life (since 18) has been revolved around people giving me their tips. Little tips, big tips, and jingly tips. Jingly tips are the worst. I have begged people for their tips. I have been politely offered their tips. I have refused a person's tip if it was too small but have never turned down a big tip. I know this is not my lifelong career, just ten to possibly 20 years of my life, and I wanted to thank you all for the funding you have all contributed these past ten years without knowing it. In all reality, I love the service industry. I basically grew up in it. You really get to see people for who they are and encounter so many different personalities on any given night. You also make a lot of great connections. Working in the service industry is a perfect way to network. I have received multiple job offers and made some of my lifelong friends working in the industry. However, in the last few years, I have given up my waitressing sneakers for bartending tools instead. I have been a high-volume bartender for the last few years and if you think these stories were good from the front line, then I can't wait to share with you the stories that come from behind the bar. Yes, I have a feeling this is just the tip of what awaits me.

SERVER TERMS AND MEANINGS

Dead- "It's so dead tonight!" You feel dead.

Actual meaning: Slow, no customers in sight, no money in sight.

Cut- "You're cut!" Your manager just cut you with a butcher's knife because you are no longer needed.

Actual meaning: You are done with your shift for the night because business is slow, and you can now start your side work.

Behind- "Behind you!" Prepare to have someone behind you.... with clothes on, of course.

Actual meaning: This means that somebody has their hands full behind you and cannot push you out of the way.

Hands- "We need hands!" This is where you show your manager your hands. They like employees with hands.

Actual meaning: We need help in the kitchen for running food or drinks to a table.

Food Runners- We all grab food and have races.

Actual meaning: We need people to WALK food to customers' tables.

86- A random number that looks appealing on paper.

Actual meaning: 86 is when you no longer have that item. "We are 86ed on Tuna tonight!"

Double- "I have to work a double today." Working double the time of a normal person in hopes to make the same amount of money as a normal person.

Actual meaning: A double is two shifts in one day.

Weeded- "I'm so weeded." You have gotten so high that you are now using weed as an uncommon adjective.

Actual meaning: You have too many tables, you have lost control, you are officially sucking and need help.

POS- Piece Of Shit computer system. Computers that you use to put in customers' orders.

COMP- "I need you to comp something for me." Comp means to have a manager get rid of something on a check either due to server error, because you spilled a food item or drink on the floor or on somebody else, or because somebody is simply refusing to pay for something they ordered.

Ramekin- A small plastic or ceramic dish used for condiments such as ketchup to serve on the plate beside a burger. When a restaurant wants to look fancier than giving you a squeezable ketchup bottle, they might provide you with a ramekin of ketchup instead.

Bank- When you make shit ton of money. I made Bank tonight!

ABOUT THE AUTHOR

Tonya Fritch is a service industry veteran currently based out of Raleigh, NC. With nearly twenty years in the industry, Tonya has had the opportunity to work in an array of restaurants, bars and nightclubs. Tonya continues to bartend while writing hilarious stories about basic human failing especially when everybody' s good friend, alcohol is involved. Tonya is currently working on her second book which dives a little deeper into the bartending industry.

WWW.TONYAFRITCH.COM
@TONYA.FRITCH

Made in the USA
Columbia, SC
30 April 2021

36568389R00115